TOWNSHIP OF UNION
FREE PUBLIC LIBRARY

The World's Best Poetry

Supplement IV

Minority Poetry of America; An Anthology of Asian, Black, Hispanic and Native American Poetry

Poetry Anthology Press

The World's Best Poetry

Volume	I	Home and Friendship
	II	Love
	III	Sorrow and Consolation
	IV	The Higher Life
	V	Nature
	VI	Fancy and Sentiment
	VII	Descriptive and Narrative
	VIII	National Spirit
	IX	Tragedy and Humor
	X	Poetical Quotations; General Indexes
Supplement	I	Twentieth Century English and American Verse, 1900–1929
	II	Twentieth Century English and American Verse, 1930–1950
	III	Critical Companion
	IV	Minority Poetry of America

Survey of American Poetry

Volume	I	Colonial Period, 1607–1765
	II	Revolutionary Era, 1766–1799
	III	Early 19th Century, 1800–1829
	IV	First Great Period, 1830–1860
	V	Civil War and Aftermath, 1861–1889
	VI	Twilight Interval, 1890–1912
	VII	Poetic Renaissance, 1913–1919
	VIII	Interval Between World Wars, 1920–1939
	IX	World War II and Aftermath, 1940–1950
	X	Midcentury to 1984; General Indexes
Annual	1985	Annual Survey of American Poetry

The World's Best Poetry

Supplement IV

Minority Poetry of America; An Anthology of Asian, Black, Hispanic and Native American Poetry

Prepared by
The Editorial Board, Roth Publishing, Inc.
(formerly Granger Book Co., Inc.)
In consultation with Konstantin Dierks

Poetry Anthology Press
Great Neck, New York

Copyright © 1987 Roth Publishing, Inc.
All rights reserved

The acknowledgements on pages 368–374
constitute a continuation of this copyright
notice.

Library of Congress Catalog Number 82-84763
International Standard Book Number 0-89609-265-8

Manufactured in the U.S.A.

Poetry Anthology Press is a
division of Roth Publishing, Inc.
(formerly Granger Book Co., Inc.)

CONTENTS

Preface xvii
Introduction xviii

Asian American Poetry

LAWSON FUSAO INADA
The Source 2
The Legendary Storm 3
Plucking Out Rhythm 4

ALEX KUO
Did You Not See 6
Portrait of a Negative 7

MEI-MEI BERSSENBRUGGE
Poor Mouse 10
Fish and Swimmers and Lonely Birds Sweep Past Us 11
Spring Street Bar 12

SHAWN WONG
Love Among Friends 13
Kicking Lego Blocks, selections 14

JESSICA HAGEDORN
Sorcery 22

Song for My Father 24
The Song of the Bullets 29

LAUREEN MAR
The Window Frames the Moon 32
Black Rocks 33
My Mother, Who Came from China,
    Where She Never Saw Snow 34

KIMIKO HAHN
Daughter 35
The Bath: August 6, 1945 36

JANICE MIRIKITANI
August 6 39
Hospitals Are to Die In 42
Desert Flowers 44

Black American Poetry

FOLK SONGS
Go Down, Moses 48
Swing Low, Sweet Chariot 50
Steal Away 51
Song 52
Many a Thousand Die 52
Song to the Runaway Slave 53
John Henry 54
She Hugged Me and Kissed Me 59
Were You There When They Crucified My Lord? 60

PHILLIS WHEATLEY
On Being Brought From Africa to America 61
An Hymn to the Evening 62

FRANCES E.W. HARPER
The Slave Auction 63

W.E.B. DU BOIS
The Song of the Smoke 65

JAMES WELDON JOHNSON
O Black and Unknown Bards 67
Let My People Go 68

PAUL LAURENCE DUNBAR
We Wear the Mask 75
The Debt 76
Little Brown Baby 77
Ere Sleep Comes Down to Soothe the Weary Eyes 78
When Malindy Sings 79

ALICE DUNBAR-NELSON
I Sit and Sew 82

GEORGIA DOUGLAS JOHNSON
The Heart of a Woman 83
I Want to Die While You Love Me 84

FENTON JOHNSON
Tired 85

CLAUDE MCKAY
The Tropics in New York 86
In Bondage 87

JEAN TOOMER
Reapers 88
Georgia Dusk 89
Song of the Son 90
Brown River, Smile 91

MELVIN B. TOLSON
Dark Symphony 96
African China 101

FRANK HORNE
Walk 106
Notes Found Near a Suicide 108

STERLING BROWN
Strange Legacies 117
Strong Men 119

ARNA BONTEMPS
Close Your Eyes! 122
Southern Mansion 123
The Return 124
A Black Man Talks of Reaping 126
Nocturne at Bethesda 127

LANGSTON HUGHES
Jazzonia 129
The Negro Speaks of Rivers 130

I, Too, Sing America 131
Dream Deferred 132
Freedom 133

COUNTEE CULLEN
Yet I Do Marvel 134

ROBERT HAYDEN
O Daedalus, Fly Away Home 135
Homage to the Empress of the Blues 136
Frederick Douglass 137
In the Mourning Time 138
The Night-Blooming Cereus 139
Middle Passage 142
Those Winter Sundays 149
Runagate Runagate 150
The Prisoners 153

DUDLEY RANDALL
Legacy: My South 154
The Southern Road 155

GWENDOLYN BROOKS
When You Have Forgotten Sunday: The Love Story 156
The Bean Eaters 158
The Sermon on the Warpland 159
The Second Sermon on the Warpland 160
Life for My Child Is Simple and Good 162

NAOMI LONG MADGETT
Mortality 163
Midway 164

Simple 165
Black Woman 166

DEREK WALCOTT
Upstate 167

ETHERIDGE KNIGHT
The Idea of Ancestry 169
He Sees Through Stone 171
It Was a Funky Deal 173

AMIRI BARAKA (LEROI JONES)
The Insidious Dr. Fu Manchu 174
The Liar 175
Cold Term 176
Jitterbugs 177
A Poem Some People Will Have to Understand 178
Young Soul 179

AUDRE LORDE
Coal 180
Summer Oracle 182
The Woman Thing 184

BOB KAUFMAN
To My Son Parker, Asleep in the Next Room 185

SONIA SANCHEZ
Right On: White America 187
Last Poem I'm Gonna Write About Us 189
Poem at Thirty 190

Poem No. 4.	191
Pennsylvania Dutch Country	192

LUCILLE CLIFTON
Good Times	193

JUNE JORDAN
All the World Moved	194
For Christopher	195
Roman Poem Number Thirteen	196
About the Reunion	197

CLARENCE MAJOR
Waiting in the Children's Hospital	199
Form	201
None of It Was	202
Dismal Moment, Passing	203
Vietnam	204

MICHAEL HARPER
We Assume: On the Death of Our Son, Reuben Masai Harper.	205

DAVID HENDERSON
Walk with De Mayor of Harlem	207

DON L. LEE
Mixed Sketches	210
Assassination	212
We Walk the Way of the New World	213
But He Was Cool	216

NIKKI GIOVANNI

A Certain Peace 218
When I Nap 219
The Women Gather 220
Revolutionary Dreams 222
Mother's Habits 223

ALICE WALKER

Expect Nothing 224
Burial 225
New Face 228
Medicine 229

NTOZAKE SHANGE

For Colored Girls Who Have Considered Suicide
   When the Rainbow Is Enuf, selections 230

Hispanic American Poetry

RODOLFO GONZALES

I Am Joaquin, selections 234

FRANK LIMA

In Medias Res 241
159 John Street 242
Vacations 243
Summer Wish 244
Hunter Mountain 245
Yellowstone 247
Plena 248

RICARDO SÁNCHEZ
Toward 249
I Remember 254

PEDRO PIETRI
Song Without Words 256
Do Not Let 258

ALMA VILLANUEVA
To Jesus Villanueva, with Love 259
Untitled 263
I Was Always Fascinated 266

MIGUEL PIÑERO
There Is Nothing New in New York 268

ALURISTA
What for?/ pa' victor hara 270
In the Barrio 274
When Raza? 275

VICTOR HERNANDEZ CRUZ
Today Is a Day of Great Joy 276
Snag 278

ALEIDA RODRÍGUEZ
Exploraciones Bronchitis: The Rosario Beach House 279

MIGUEL ALGARÍN
Sunday, August 11, 1974 283

TERESA PALOMO ACOSTA
My Mother Pieced Quilts 285

AMERICO CASIANO
When Was the Last Time You Saw Mami Smile? 288

CARLOS CONDE
That's How I Was 291

SANDRA MARIA ESTEVES
Blanket Weaver 292

Native American Poetry

NORMAN RUSSELL
The Tree Sleeps in the Winter 296
There Is a Hungry Watching 297

JIM BARNES
Last Look at La Plata, Missouri 298
Lost in Sulphur Canyons 299

N. SCOTT MOMADAY
Carriers of the Dream Wheels 301
Earth and I Gave You Turquoise 302

DUANE NIATUM
Chief Leschi of the Nisqually 303

PAULA GUNN ALLEN
Grandmother 304
Kopis'taya (a Gathering of Spirits) 305

ROBERT J. CONLEY
The Rattlesnake Band. 307
We Wait 309

JAMES WELCH
Blue Like Death 312

SIMON ORTIZ
Survival This Way 314
The Serenity in Stones 315
What I Tell Him 316
To Insure Survival 317

JOSEPH BRUCHAC
Coming Back 318

GLADYS CARDIFF
Long Person 319
Combing 321

LIZ SOHAPPY BAHE
Farewell 322

WENDY ROSE
Halfbreed Cry 323
Story Keeper 325

LESLIE MARMON SILKO
Toe'osh: A Laguna Coyote Story 328
Indian Song: Survival. 331
The Time We Climbed Snake Mountain 334
Where Mountain Lion Lay with Deer 335
Love Poem 336

RAY A. YOUNG BEAR
The Way the Bird Sat 337

JOY HARJO
Someone Talking 339
3 AM 342

Biographical Notes 343

Index 361

PREFACE

The publications of **Poetry Anthology Press** constitute a comprehensive conspectus of international verse in English designed to form the core of a library's poetry collection. Covering the entire range of poetic literature, these anthologies encompass all topics and national literatures.

Each collection, published in a multivolume continuing series format, is devoted to a major area of the whole undertaking and contains complete author, title, and first line indexes. Biographical data is also provided.

The World's Best Poetry, with coverage through the 19th century, is topically classified and arranged by subject matter. *Supplements* keep this 10 volume foundation collection current and complete.

Survey of American Poetry is an anthology of American verse arranged chronologically in 10 volumes. Each volume presents a significant period of American poetic history, from 1607 to date. *Annual Survey of American Poetry* serves to keep the foundation set timely.

INTRODUCTION

Poetry by minority Americans—Asian Americans, Black Americans, Hispanic Americans, and Native Americans—has long been neglected in the United States. The poetry has not received due exposure in literary journals, in published collections, and in most anthologies. This anthology is specifically intended to acknowledge and appreciate the many talented minority poets who have written and are writing outside the cultural and literary mainstream in the United States.

Poetry can be loosely defined as the verbal expression of cultural perspective and personal identity. Poetry by minority Americans commonly expresses a conscious attempt to preserve the dignity of their own unique cultural heritages, heritages that threaten to be lost as each generation assimilates more fully into American mainstream culture. The poetry concentrates on cultural preservation through a variety of literary themes. Robert Hayden, for example, is known for his historical narratives on the enslavement of Blacks in the United States, while Rodolfo Gonzales gained renown for creating an epic that recounts the history of and the injustices faced by Chicanos in Mexico and in the United States.

Many of the poems center on the family as parents and grandparents come to represent the poet's cultural heritage. Janice Mirikitani's work is deeply concerned with the effect that the atomic bomb dropped on Hiroshima had on her mother and, by extension, on her own attitudes. The poetry may also plead with the children of the poets to learn and to continue their cultural heritage. Simon Ortiz's work often exhorts his children to respect the Indian folk tradition and to hold a reverence for nature. This approach to poetic sensibility has been termed "cultural nationalism."

Although cultural nationalism is a major theme in the poetry of minority writers, an inescapable motif that abounds in the poetry is the injustices which are faced by minorities in America. All minorities have encountered realities far removed from the fundamental American promise of freedom and opportunity for all. Poverty and prejudice have afflicted minority groups in the United States from the country's inception. Asian Americans, Black Americans, Hispanic Americans, and Native Americans, specifically, have been subject to systematic oppression and brutal violence, and were long denied the fundamental rights of citizenship.

The prejudice against minorities is bitterly felt in the poetry. The poetry often expresses frustration and protest against the social reality of life for minorities. It constantly excoriates and challenges the cultural and political assumptions of the dominant mainstream cultural traditions. One manifestation of this challenging is the conscious digression from the ordinary language habits of American society. For this reason, David Henderson uses fractured syntax, Alurista writes bilingual poetry, and Victor Cruz uses "street" idioms.

The poetry is often direct and sometimes plainly didactic in the expression of its bitterness. It uses minimal artifices of understatement, irony, and metaphor which characterize much mainstream American poetry. (Exceptions are Frank Lima and Clarence Major in this anthology.) This bitterness is framed by cultural nationalism, since cultural identity is thrust upon the poetry by daily reminders of prejudice against minorities and pervasive signs of poverty among minorities in the United States.

Many of the poets have devoted much of their time as social activists or spokespersons for their groups. Amiri Baraka and Alice Walker, for example, both have been active community organizers. Robert Conley has served as a leader of the Cherokee Nation in Oklahoma. Ricardo Sánchez and Alurista have been leading activists in the Chicano movement in the Southwest United States. Shawn Wong and Kimiko Hahn have expended great effort to academic projects for the benefit of Asian Americans.

This dedication to cultural nationalism has raised accusations by many literary critics that minority American poets do not write with sufficient universal perspective. On the other hand, the poets are accused of not writing with enough of a racial/ethnic consciousness by their minority peers. The dilemma facing minority American poets is, at the surface, whether to place cultural perspective, or personal sensibility, first. However, on closer examination, this turns out to be an unfair choice. Cultural nationalism is undoubtedly prominent in much of the poetry, but this is a reflex against the persistent injustice felt by minorities. Moreover, while cultural perspective is effectively submerged in mainstream American poetry, it is not entirely absent. Poetry cannot insulate itself from its social relevance, nor from its ability to achieve empathy with a wide and diverse audience. Poetry which sways too far to one side, either cultural perspective or personal sensibility, narrows its focus prohibitively, alienating audiences and losing its efficacy.

The difficulty facing minority American poets is even more complicated for those poets who are also women. Minority women experience a compounded prejudice in mainstream American society—both as members of a minority and as women. Feminism has become an important component of the more recent poetry by minority American women poets. It may compete with or even supplant racial/ethnic consciousness. This is true of the work of Ntozake Shange and Alma Villaneuva, for example.

The emergence of poetry by minority Americans has been dependent on a number of factors. In 1896 Paul Laurence Dunbar's *Lyrics of a Lowly Life* was the first poetry collection by a Black American to be produced by a major publisher; however, it was only after World War I, during the so-called Harlem Renaissance, that a few Black poets received national recognition for their poetic accomplishment. In 1922, with the publication of James Weldon Johnson's seminal anthology, *The Book of American Negro Poetry*, Black American poets received more serious and proper recognition. For Native Americans, Hispanic Americans, and Asian Americans, it required the ramifications of the civil rights movement of the 1960s to foster some due recognition. *I Am Joaquin* by Rodolfo Gonzales, published in 1967, is considered the first major poetry collection by a Hispanic American in the United States. Lawson Inada's *Before the War*, published in 1971, was the first poetry collection by an Asian American to be produced by a major publisher.

The emergence of small journals and presses willing to publish poetry by minority Americans is an important factor in bringing minority poetry to a larger audience. For example, the Greenfield Review founded by Joseph Bruchac has been exemplary in publishing writings by minority Americans. The Broadside Press founded by Dudley Randall has been a major outlet for Black American writings.

The importance of anthologies of minority American poetry also cannot be underestimated. This anthology represents an attempt to broaden the tradition of American poetry by separately featuring the work of minority Americans. Hopefully, once minority American poetry and its unique characteristics achieve their due recognition and appreciation, it can be properly incorporated as integral to and inseparable from the American poetic tradition without the "minority" distinction. Minority American poets have already made important contributions to the poetic tradition in the United States; it is past time that these contributions be acknowledged and appreciated.

ASIAN AMERICAN POETRY

Lawson Fusao Inada

The Source

Bare
hills, cross-
legged, brush
in the folds
moist
into summer
and the drought.
Rivers
are cold.
Sand,
too hot
to hold
gives
to my motion.
Hawks
in the sky—
something
burnt
and floating.

The Legendary Storm

A legendary storm—that's
what I wanted—a bad
blizzard coming down,
covering me like a legendary
hat—nine big feathers
and a five-inch brim.
That year, we lived in a long house,
eaves like wings, icicle
feathers keeping me in.

This year we've got a cheap flat
with skinny curtains.
The storms come in
when they please.
And there's a big bad bear
snarling around the corner.
He's got a sad face and grey
around his collar. He's
a mountain; I'm
me. Please

send me a child to love.

Plucking Out a Rhythm

Start with a simple room—
a dullish color—
and draw the one shade down.
Hot plate. Bed.
Little phonograph in a corner.

Put in a single figure—
medium weight and height—
but oversize, as a child might.

The features must be Japanese.

Then stack a black pompadour on,
and let the eyes
slide behind a night of glass.

The figure is in disguise:

slim green suit
for posturing on a bandstand,
the turned-up shoes of Harlem . . .

Then start the music playing—
thick jazz, strong jazz—

and notice that the figure
comes to life:

sweating, growling
over an imaginary bass—
plucking out a rhythm—
as the music rises and the room is full,
exuding with that rhythm . . .

Then have the shade flap up
and daylight catch him
frozen in that pose

as it starts to snow—
thick snow, strong snow—

blowing in the window
while the music quiets,
the room is slowly covered,

and the figure is completely
out of sight.

Alex Kuo

Did You Not See

the aspens yesterday
intolerant and drawn
together high up on the Divide?

Perhaps you gave them a glance
gazing out the high window
in the back of your house
saw nothing and now
remember nothing more?

What did the second settlers
see when they first stumbled
up these yellowed tiers
trying to find their way to
the Pacific, their senses drying
in that October trying
to change their significance?

Perhaps now you can remember
their prints in that early ice
how they packed along their dead
until the ground was soft
enough for late burial
step after step
disappearing high into
this incomprehensible blue.

Portrait of a Negative

1.
Limping to this spreading portrait
we came

the ill, some saints, the perverse, and
a few

with historical names, searching for
the flaw.

2.
With tears drowning in the night
overhead fan breaking black
glass, I search for originals
of negatives, black and white
plates of my grandparents, death
experts in their own right.

3.
The eye sees little that the mind
has not

known before: a hole in the wall
the blood

spreading down the bed, arrivals
departures.

4.
Their pools of blood settle
about my feet, closing
door shutting out sunlight
from abyss of bed slept

disinterestedly
inward after the murder
of love's lovemaking.

5.
Tell me this isn't so. Tell me
as I

stand near my own body, watching
old men

in their eccentric lie. Tell me
as I

watch this blood pulsing out of me.
Tell me.

6.
I can almost see
a bleached bird perched in
the distance where the
sun is limp and still
farther small bits of
yellowed photographs
showing the reverse
of what must have once
been true and oh yes
devoured and destroyed
even though perhaps
they came the closest.

7.
They are standing about me now
watching

trying to preserve some knowledge
for their

future, trying to retain an
image

of the past, of me, standing still
watching

me watching them, disregarding
that what

they now see as changeless was
never.

8.
light breaks in this prism
of the past guilt gnaws away
at flesh distant sound of
gunfire bodies fall apart
and I just want to lie
down in the blood and drowning
in my own body no
portrait to hold monument

Mei-mei Berssenbrugge

Poor Mouse

We took the mouse alive
from the trap
and washed his cheek
and set him under some leaves
with a chicken bone by Ordway's gate
In the morning we found him crushed flat
by some heavy thing

When small creatures die
we are not to feel for them
They flow down into the river
and the ones crazed find a way
to live again

according to the weather
the horsetails and the wind:
in the cakepan
in the woodshed
in the hemlock trees
I hear a vibration fading away
but I never hear the thing striking.

Fish and Swimmers and Lonely Birds Sweep Past Us

Today I love you so much I mistrust you -
our future bows out and swells
like liquid and falls under a bird's wing

each day runs after the other days
joining them with its tiny body
and heartbeats

Our bodies
lean toward center when we walk
sealed in a floating bell
phosphorus lighting up our eyes

and the bell is ringing
fish and swimmers
and lonely birds sweep by all around us

- and I look at you and you're invisible

Spring Street Bar

And last night a man came in
to tell her of stars and clouds moving fast
though the day itself had been dark and thick
when she tried to write to George, at first
without paper, which worked fine from Mercer Street
where bits of cloth and poisonous gas held letter
shapes well, but in the sheer air over his house
words ascended instead of entering the chimney
clearly marked by smoke. He was baking bread
with the yellow dog napping beside him
Each word rose on an updraft the hawk used, too
then dissolved among ghosts of indians and fish
when the poisons were flushed down by snow

She knew about ghosts and also the hawk
they had watched rise without moving at the edge
of the plain, until it was gone. Then she asked
could he still see it, to hear *yes* and watch
his blue eyes scan space. The trail to the ruin
had seemed to crumble under her feet. Handholds
pocked with braille instead of rain had warned her
So she took some paper and began as she used to
when there had been a sky, to write about the sky

Shawn Wong

Love among Friends

In trust you showed me a photograph
of a ragged girl with long black hair
cradling a wounded baby.
She pretends to whisper rhymes to her sister
saying all the time, "Renew these bones."
Calmly, you tell me that there are places
where children
have learned to lie down like tigers
and watch for the fire,
the blue fire.

Then you asked me to understand your spirit
because of love among friends.
To carry the wounded children,
to cradle their blue arms in mine.
Spring passes by in a moment of dreams
and we too have learned to sleep like tigers
to watch for the fire that is precious
blue and ceaselessly blue.

Being a mother you said
that you would pay for everything
not in guilt, but by commitment.
You must dream at night of your own
children lost in a world of red clouds.

Kicking Lego Blocks, Selections

1.

Two hours after I saw her
at 2 a.m., June 28th, 1972
Cindy sat down to write to me,
"So much to do
I had to push aside paper piles
and write this to you."

And it was all of me
in the poem.

And I also went home
at midnight after seeing you
to write back to you
to say something about my father
because you put me back in touch
with myself
left me thinking and seeing
a dream out of the clear night
until it started raining
and you were home
giving me the day
as it comes from the heart
so full of sun
even writing about the day:

"The dogs are barking
I must go outside into the sun bleached day now
Kicking Lego blocks and mini trucks from steps,
To tug on dry crackling grass with clawing roots
From around my big wooden house
Before that fire next time."

This is only the beginning
and you watch me now
as I make my life up from friends
what they've given me.

And I'm always driving,
pulling myself up by my arms
to see and create
to chronicle everything that I am
for you
so that you will see me growing.

II.

Wherever we are in this country
you and I are still thinking
about each other.
Cindy in Miami, San Diego,
even from Vienna you wrote to me.

I was in the mountains
always sending postcards
from places I've never been to before.
And maybe someday we'll
be in the same place together
sending cards home
from some windy place
from some home that gives
our families to us
from old old buildings where we used to live
from an island
where you are taking me
to show me where your grandmother survived

where you'll say to me
that all she wanted was a place to live

and you'll show me a window
that I can look out
and see my own home
and hear nothing except the broken glass
under your shoes
keeping time with your voice saying,
"We'll make them all remember I swear,
We'll stake out this place and unleash the ghosts."

The windows are broken and open
for Cindy's ghosts to fly through
tearing the sill to shreds.
No splinters come from this rotting wood
Cindy passes through
and walks lightly to hear
voices rise up to greet her
like me listening for my father's voice
move through the floor
at the radio station
Cindy becomes blind
to hear only
to run her fingers across
poems
carved into the walls
with fingers like Cindy's.
"Staying on this island
My sorrow increases with the days
My face is growing sallow
And my body is getting thin
Cooped up here, my difficulties are unending
Now, I dare to give up all and go back."
We will never go back
We will root ourselves in place
on this land
Cindy will see to it
because these buildings breathe

because this whole island is a heart
beating
"Ask the Indians they'll all tell you,"
Cindy says,
"that an island is the saddest
kind of land there is."
We do unleash ghosts now
that fill all the homes
and Cindy still cries
but she's mad now
so we take hold
of this stronghold
to chronicle all that is rising
up to greet us
in Cindy's fire

VIII.

Breakfast at Cindy's place
is full of smiles
like Marty marching off to school
with his briefcase,
the dogs are crying
at his leaving
and we are left alone in your house
to realize that Marty goes off
to do so many things at school
with his life
and we're at home
relaxed, talking projects,
making moves to control what we do
while Marty grabs what he sees
protects what he learns
uses what he learns
to create everything that he will be.

And we are already
recording things
making lists of what we have been
or what we will be to each other
to our friends
or even, to nations of people
we don't even know.

But the music is on
And Cindy is making
Italian enchiladas filled with Spam
sprinkled with cheese
for breakfast,
hot Viennese Blend coffee,
and after breakfast
we have Cindy's omelet bread
made with chicken and duck eggs
from the coop,
macaroons the size of fists,
and San Miguel Beer
to ruin the rest of the day.

By June 1972
Cindy had written that poem for me
knowing me only three months
and I wrote back a month later
giving Cindy my poem for her
in a letter saying,
"Dear Cindy, I have finished your poem.
I struggled to see the vision that holds the poem,
but breaks the person —
excuse me if I have given you a harsher vision
or a harsher dream about the children
of Southeast Asia than you might have.
It makes the point.
There are certain problems

with the poem that I will work out
in the next few weeks;
(1) 'red clouds' interrupts
the images of blue,
and (2) I am wondering if 'commitment'
just before is strong enough."

I must have known Cindy longer
to know that wasn't strong enough
in fact, nothing *said* is strong enough
only the working
the *doing*
matters to Cindy
and so I looked back at what I said
about Cindy
about all that love among friends
and still felt what I said
mattered because it was for Cindy.
I looked back to March 25, 1971
when Kay dedicated a poem for me,
with love, saying,
"Once into this curse of reading, one learns there are places
Named My Song, My Lai, and also the other tramplings to death,
The assault upon leaves, roots, small vines with their palms
    open. . ."
I never corrected the poem for Cindy
but wrote back to her
on September 16, 1972
to say something I had been feeling
all along:
" . . . your simple note settled me,
nothing to jump for joy about,
or anything that obvious,
or gaudy,
but a happiness surrounded by simplicity
that is implied in the definition of the action,

Kindness.
Ever, ever is another word
that moves like a song
exposes the heart in its tone,
never hides, never patronizes.
The word speaks directly, creates form,
has its own voice.
Now I am telling you that words
speak for themselves,
out of control.
But ever is stronger than commitment."

Now I have put all of that
into the story about me
the long work
about a home on the range
that is mine
that is everything my heart wants
and together we never
needed much
because we were always
giving something to each other
Cindy has always
given me small cups, pots,
shirts, food,
useful things
like we were in exile together
needing supplies
like letters

Like now
to build
to carve
all that we want
at the marrow
where our blood clings

where it will pulse out of the bone
when needed
to invade an island
of people we knew,
to protect friends,
to find words like genocide
come pulsing out of our mouths
in a voice strong
as the bone it flows from
because we've seen children
wear their flesh like loose clothing.
Maybe they're all dead now
and maybe the children still there
will die from a war
that still goes on

within them
because they're still looking
for homes, for food,
that will take years to grow
out of their own land
but Cindy will continue to cry
over some soldier-father
who died years ago
simply because he missed his family
his life continues for her
will come back to her
especially on hot days like today

Jessica Hagedorn

Sorcery

there are some people i know
whose beauty is a crime.
who make you so crazy
you don't know
whether to throw yourself
at them
or kill them.
you better be on the lookout
for such circumstances.

stay away
from the night.
they most likely lurk
in corners of the room
where they think
they being inconspicuous
but they so beautiful
an aura
gives them away.

stay away
from the day.
they most likely
be walking down the street
trying to look ordinary
but they so fine
they break your heart

by making you dream
of other possibilities.

stay away
from crazy music.
they most likely be
creating it.
cuz when you're that beautiful
you can't help
putting it out there.
everyone knows
how dangerous
that can get.

stay away
from magic shows.
especially those
involving words.
words are very tricky things.
everyone knows
words the most common
instruments of illusion.

they most likely
be saying them.
breathing poems
so rhythmic
you can't help but dance.

and once
you start dancing
to words

you might
never stop.

Song for My Father

i arrive
in the unbearable heat
the sun's stillness
stretching across
the land's silence
people staring out
from airport cages
thousands of miles later
and i have not yet understood
my obsession to return

and twelve years
is fast
inside my brain
exploding like tears
i could show you
but you already know.

you greet me
and i see
it is you
you all the time
pulling me back
towards this space

letters are the memory
i carry with me
the unspoken name
of you,
my father

in new york
they ask me

if i'm puerto rican
and do i live in queens?
i listen to pop stations chant
to iemaja
convinced i'm really brazilian
and you a riverboat gambler
shooting dice in macao
during the war

roaches fly around us
like bats in twilight
and barry white grunts
in fashionable discotheques
setting the pace
for guerrillas to grind

the president's wife
has a fondness for concert pianists
and gossip
is integral to conversation

if you eat enough papaya
your sex drive diminishes
lorenza paints my nails blue
and we giggle at the dinner table
aunts and whores
brothers and homosexuals
a contessa with chinese eyes
and an uncle cranky with loneliness
he carries an american passport
like me

and here we are
cathedrals in our thighs
banana trees for breasts
and history all mixed up

saxophones in our voices
when we scream
the love of rhythms
inherent
when we dance

they can latin here
and shoot you
for the wrong glance
eyes that kill
eyes that kill

dope dealers are executed
in public
and senators go mad
in prison camps
the nightclubs are burning
with indifference
curfew drawing near
soldiers lurk in jeeps
of dawn warzones
as the president's daughter
boogies nostalgically
under the gaze
of sixteen smooth bodyguards
and decay is forever
even in the rage
of humorless revolutionaries

in hotel lobbies
we drink rum
testing each other's wit
snakes sometimes crawl
in our beds
but what can you do
in the heat

the laziness makes you love
so easily

you smile like buddha
urging me to swim with you
the water is clear
with corpses
of dragonflies and mosquitos
i'm writing different poems now
my dreams have become reptilian
and green
everything green
green and hot

eyes that kill
eyes that kill

women slither in and out
of barroom doorways
their tongues massage the terror
from your nightmares
the lizard hissing nervously
as he watches you breathe

i am trapped
by overripe mangoes
i am trapped
by the beautiful sadness of women
i am trapped
by priests and nuns
whispering my name
in confession boxes
i am trapped
by antiques and the music
of the future

and leaving you
again and again
for america
the loneliest of countries

my words change . . .
sometimes
i even forget english

The Song of Bullets

Formalized
by middle age
we avoid crowds
but still
love music.

Day after day
with less surprise
we sit
in apartments
and count
the dead.

Awake,
my daughter croons
her sudden cries
and growls
my new language.
While she sleeps
we memorize
a list of casualties:

The photographer's brother
the doctor is missing.
Or I could say:
"Victor's brother Oscar
has been gone for two years . . .
It's easier for the family
to think of him dead."

Victor sends
a Christmas card

from El Salvador:
"Things still the same."

And there are others
who don't play
by the rules—
someone else's brother
perhaps mine
languishes in a hospital;
everyone's grown tired
of his nightmares
and pretends
he's not there.

Someone else's father
perhaps mine
will be executed
when the time comes.
Someone else's mother
perhaps mine
telephones incessantly
her husband is absent
her son has gone mad
her lover has committed suicide
she's a survivor
who can't appreciate
herself.

The sight
of my daughter's
pink and luscious flesh
undoes me.
I fight
my weakening rage
I must remember
to commit

those names to memory
and stay angry.

Friends send postcards:
"Alternating between hectic
social Manila life & rural wonders
of Sagata . . . on to Hongkong and Bangkok—
Love . . . "

Assassins cruise the streets
in obtrusive limousines
sunbathers idle
on the beach

War is predicted
in five years
ten years
any day now
I always thought
it was already happening

snipers and poets locked
in a secret embrace
the country
my child may never see

a heritage
of women in heat
and men
skilled at betrayal

dancing
to the song
of bullets.

Laureen Mar

The Window Frames the Moon

Some nights the moon is the curve of a comb,
tumble of night held casually;
other nights, a plate broken perfectly in half,
box of night coveting the smooth edge.

The window frames the moon, places it
to the left of the world, to the right,
decides if it floats, hurtles, suspends,
glances, antagonizes, surrenders.

By eleven the moon is as certain and fixed
as the clock on the dresser,
the chink in the wall,
the black tablecloth with silver dots of glitter.

Every night is the opportunity to rearrange the world!
With the window, I push the moon into place
as if it were a vase of flowers.
Oh, the glory of the night contained!

But there are nights the moon looms large,
so large it refuses to fit in the frame,
so large it refuses to splinter,
and when I push the moon, it pushes back

and fills my house, and I am forced to abandon
the clock and the dresser

to stand with the trees, leaves, grass,
taking my place among the small things of the world.

Black Rocks

1.
Your mother poses on black rocks.
The sun flares white behind her.
Is it the sun that makes her dark eyes frown
this time—the camera, or the child
who waits to lean against her skirt,
the yellow jungle that promises
heat and a torrid wind?

2.
You were born on black rocks.
You climbed the jagged
face against your mother's
warning, digging your way past yellow
and white daisies, the frail iris.
From the neighbor you stole whatever
was in season, crabapples, cherries.

3.
You fall against black rocks.
The sky opens, startled
green leaves rising above you faster
than your hands. You lie in the grass
listening to your mother rushing,
your lips bleeding brightly.
Your mouth shows a faint bone-white scar.

My Mother, Who Came from China, Where She Never Saw Snow

In the huge, rectangular room, the ceiling
a machinery of pipes and fluorescent lights,
ten rows of women hunch over machines,
their knees pressing against pedals
and hands pushing the shiny fabric thick as tongues
through metal and thread.
My mother bends her head to one of these machines.
Her hair is coarse and wiry, black as burnt scrub.
She wears glasses to shield her intense eyes.
A cone of orange thread spins. Around her,
talk flutters harshly in Toisan wah.*
Chemical stings. She pushes cloth
through a pounding needle, under, around, and out,
breaks thread with a snap against fingerbone, tooth.
Sleeve after sleeve, sleeve.
It is easy. The same piece.
For eight or nine hours, sixteen bundles maybe,
250 sleeves to ski coats, all the same.
It is easy, only once she's run the needle
through her hand. She earns money
by each piece, on a good day,
thirty dollars. Twenty-four years.
It is frightening how fast she works.
She and the women who were taught sewing
terms in English as Second Language.
Dull thunder passes through their fingers.

*Toisan wah: *wah* means language; Toisan is a region of Canton province.

Kimiko Hahn

Daughter

Although I'm oldest I can't
be the one who paints

or speaks grandmother's language
like a picture-bride marriage

to a still life: a plate
of oranges, plums and grapes

one takes care to arrange
precise as syntax—as a passage

one must translate
for someone else. That

is the greater danger
than waking with a stranger.

The Bath: August 6, 1945

Bathing the summer night
off my arms and breasts
I heard a plane
overhead   *I heard*
the front door rattle
froze
then relaxed
in the cool water
one more moment
one private moment
before waking the children
and mother-in-law,
before the heat
before the midday heat
drenched my spirits again.
I had wanted
to also relax
in thoughts of my husband—
how we were children
when he was drafted
imprisoned—but didn't dare
and rose from the tub,
dried off lightly
and slipped on cotton work pants.
Caution drew me to the window
and there
an enormous blossom of fire
a hand   changed my life
and made the world shiver—
a light that tore flesh
so it slipped off limbs,
swelled so
no one could recognize

a mother or child
a hand that tore the door open
pushed me on the floor
ripped me up—
I will never have children again
so even today
my hair has not grown back
my teeth still shards
and one eye blind
and it would be easy,
satisfying somehow
to write it off as history
those men are there
each time I close
my one good eye
each time or lay blame
on men or militarists
the children cry out
in my sleep
where they still live
for the sake of a night's rest.
But it is not air raids
simply
that we survive
but *diamonds worth their value*
in blood   the coal,
oil, uranium we mine
and drill
yet cannot call our own.
And it would be gratifying
to be called a survivor
I am a survivor
since I live   if I didn't wonder
about survival today—
at 55, widowed at 18—
if I didn't feel

the same oppressive August heat
auto parts in South Africa
Mexico Alabama
and shiver not from memory
or terror
but anger that this wounded body
must stand   *take a stand*
and cry out
as only a new born baby can cry—
I live, I will live
I will to live
in spite of history
to make history
in my vision of peace—
that morning in the bath
so calm
so much my right
though I cannot return to that moment
I bring these words to you
hoping to hold you
to hold you
and to take hold.

Janice Mirikitani

August 6

Yesterday
a thousand cranes
were flying.
Hiroshima,
your children
still dying
          and they said

          it saved many lives

the great white heat
that shook flesh from bone
melted bone
to dust
          and they said
          it was merciful

yesterday
a thousand cranes
were flying.
Obachan
offered omame
to her radiant Buddha
incense smoking miniature
mushrooms
her lips moving
in prayer

for sister they found
tatooed to the ground
a fleshless shadow on Hiroshima soil

        and they said
        Nagaski

Yesterday
a woman
bore a child
with fingers
growing from her neck
shoulder
empty

        and they said
        the arms race

Today
a thousand cranes
are flying
and in expensive waiting rooms
of Hiroshima, California
are blood counts
sucked by the white death

        and they said
        it might happen again

tonight
while
everyone sleeps
memoryless
the night wind
flutters like a thousand wings
how many ears will hear

the whisper
"Hiroshima"
from a child's
armless shoulder
puckered
like a kiss?

Hospitals Are To Die In

They finally
had to take obachan
she was dying

        hospitals
        takai
            takai
        she whispered

but she is dying

when they carried her
body
barely breathing,
they were carrying my soul
wrapped in the thin sheath
of her skin.

The ambulance attendants
rushed from their
coffee break
irritated,
dropped her on the
stretcher
and bumped her
against the door
violating her sleep

She wanted to stay
die in the house
that was like a body
wrapping her
in smells she knew

breathing memories
for her.

In the corners
of her closed eyes
silent tears brimming
protesting
not the hospital

        cold
        white
        expensive

the attendants swore
as they slung
the stretcher

complaining
about the high cost of living.

One said
he had to buy a
side of beef
to hang in his freezer.

        it's cheaper that way.

Desert Flowers

Flowers
faded
in the desert wind.
No flowers grow
where dust winds blow
and rain is like
a dry heave moan.

        Mama, did you dream about that
        beau who would take you
        away from it all,
        who would show you
        in his '41 ford
        and tell you how soft
        your hands
        like the silk kimono
        you folded for the wedding?
        Make you forget
        about That place,
        the back bending
        wind that fell like a wall,
        drowned all your geraniums
        and flooded the shed
        where you tried to sleep
        away hyenas?
        And mama,
        bending in the candlelight,
        after lights out in barracks,
        an ageless shadow
        grows victory flowers
        made from crepe paper,
        shaping those petals
        like the tears

> your eyes bled.
> Your fingers
> knotted at knuckles
> wounded, winding around wire stems
> the tiny, sloganed banner:
>
> > "america for americans".
>
> Did you dream
> of the shiny ford
> (only always a dream)
> ride your youth
> like the wind
> in the headless night?

Flowers
2¢ a dozen,
flowers for American Legions
worn like a badge
on america's lapel
made in post-concentration camps
by candlelight.
Flowers
watered
by the spit
of "no japs wanted here",
planted in poverty
of postwar relocations,
plucked by
victory's veterans.

> Mama, do you dream
> of the wall of wind
> that falls
> on your limbless desert,
> on stems

                brimming with petals/crushed
                crepepaper
                growing
                from the crippled
                mouth of your hand?

Your tears, mama,
have nourished us.
Your children
like pollen
scatter in the wind.

BLACK AMERICAN POETRY

Folk Songs

Go Down, Moses

Go down, Moses,
Way down in Egyptland;
Tell old Pharaoh
To let my people go.

When Israel was in Egyptland,
Let my people go.
Oppressed so hard they could not stand,
Let my people go.

Go down, Moses,
Way down in Egyptland;
Tell old Pharaoh,
"Let my people go."

"Thus saith the Lord," bold Moses said,
"Let my people go:
If not I'll smite your first-born dead,
Let my people go."

"No more shall they in bondage toil,
    Let my people go;
Let them come out with Egypt's spoil,
    Let my people go."

The Lord told Moses what to do,
    Let my people go;

To lead the children of Israel through,
   Let my people go.

Go down, Moses,
   Way down in Egyptland;
Tell old Pharaoh,
   "Let my people go!"

Swing Low, Sweet Chariot

Swing low, sweet chariot,
Coming for to carry me home,
Swing low, sweet chariot,
Coming for to carry me home.

I looked over Jordan and what did I see
Coming for to carry me home,
A band of angels, coming after me,
Coming for to carry me home.

If you get there before I do,
Coming for to carry me home,
Tell all my friends I'm coming too,
Coming for to carry me home.

Swing low, sweet chariot,
Coming for to carry me home,
Swing low, sweet chariot,
Coming for to carry me home.

Steal Away

Steal away, steal away, steal away to Jesus,
Steal away, steal away home,
I ain't got long to stay here.

My Lord, He calls me,
He calls me by the thunder,
The trumpet sounds within-a my soul,
I ain't got long to stay here.

Steal away, steal away, steal away to Jesus,
Steal away, steal away home,
I ain't got long to stay here.

Green trees a-bending,
Po' sinner stands a-trembling
The trumpet sounds within-a my soul,
I ain't got long to stay here.

Song

(From FREDERICK DOUGLASS, *My Bondage and My Freedom*, 1853)

We raise de wheat,
Dey gib us de corn:
We bake de bread,
Dey gib us de crust;
We sif de meal,
Dey gib us de huss;
We peel de meat,
Dey gib us de skin;
And dat's de way
Dey take us in;
We skim de pot,
Dey gib us de liquor,
And say dat's good enough for nigger.

Many a Thousand Die

No more driver call for me,
    No more driver call;
No more driver call for me,
    Many a thousand die!
No more peck of corn for me,
    No more peck of corn;
No more peck of corn for me,
    Many a thousand die!
No more hundred lash for me,
    No more hundred lash;
No more hundred lash for me,
    Many a thousand die!

Song to the Runaway Slave

Go 'way from dat window, "My Honey, My Love!"
Go 'way from dat window! I say.
De baby's in de bed, an' his mammy's lyin' by,
But you cain't git yo' lodgin' here.

Go 'way from dat window, "My Honey, My Love!"
Go 'way from dat window! I say;
Fer ole Mosser's got 'is gun, an' to Miss'ip' youse been
    sol';
So you cain't git yo' lodgin' here.

Go 'way from dat window, "My Honey, My Love!"
Go 'way from dat window! I say.
De baby keeps a-cryin'; but you'd better un'erstan'
Dat you cain't git yo' lodgin' here.

Go 'way from dat window, "My Honey, My Love!"
Go 'way from dat window! I say;
Fer de Devil's in dat man, an' you'd better un'erstan'
Dat you cain't git yo' lodgin' here.

John Henry

When John Henry was a little fellow,
   You could hold him in the palm of your hand,
He said to his pa, "When I grow up
   I'm gonna be a steel-driving man.
      Gonna be a steel-driving man."

When John Henry was a little baby,
   Setting on his mammy's knee,
He said "The Big Bend Tunnel on the C. & O. Road
   Is gonna be the death of me,
      Gonna be the death of me."

One day his captain told him,
   How he had bet a man
That John Henry would beat his steam drill down,
   Cause John Henry was the best in the land,
      John Henry was the best in the land.

John Henry kissed his hammer,
   White man turned on steam,
Shaker held John Henry's trusty steel,
   Was the biggest race the world had ever seen,
      Lord, biggest race the world ever seen.

John Henry on the right side
   The steam drill on the left,
"Before I'll let your steam drill beat me down,
   I'll hammer my fool self to death,
      Hammer my fool self to death."

John Henry walked in the tunnel,
   His captain by his side,
The mountain so tall, John Henry so small,

He laid down his hammer and he cried,
    Laid down his hammer and he cried.

Captain heard a mighty rumbling.
    Said "The mountain must be caving in,
John Henry said to the captain,
    "It's my hammer swinging in de wind,
        My hammer swinging in de wind."

John Henry said to his shaker,
    "Shaker, you'd better pray;
For if ever I miss this piece of steel,
    Tomorrow'll be your burial day,
        Tomorrow'll be your burial day."

John Henry said to his shaker,
    "Lordy, shake it while I sing,
I'm pulling my hammer from my shoulders down,
    Great Gawdamighty, how she ring,
        Great Gawdamighty, how she ring!"

John Henry said to his captain,
    "Before I ever leave town,
Gimme one mo' drink of dat tom-cat gin,
    And I'll hammer dat steam driver down,
        I'll hammer dat steam driver down."

John Henry said to his captain,
    "Before I ever leave town,
Gimme a twelve-pound hammer wid a whale-bone handle,
    And I'll hammer dat steam driver down,
        I'll hammer dat steam drill on down."

John Henry said to his captain,
    "A man ain't nothin' but a man,
But before I'll let dat steam drill beat me down,

I'll die wid my hammer in my hand,
    Die wid my hammer in my hand."

The man that invented the steam drill
    He thought he was mighty fine,
John Henry drove down fourteen feet,
    While the steam drill only made nine,
        Steam drill only made nine.

"Oh, lookaway over yonder, captain,
    You can't see like me,"
He gave a long and loud and lonesome cry,
    "Lawd, a hammer be the death of me,
        A hammer be the death of me!"

John Henry had a little woman,
    Her name was Polly Ann,
John Henry took sick, she took his hammer,
    She hammered like a natural man,
        Lawd, she hammered like a natural man.

John Henry hammering on the mountain
    As the whistle blew for half-past two,
The last words his captain heard him say,
    "I've done hammered my insides in two,
        Lawd, I've hammered my insides in two."

The hammer that John Henry swung
    It weighed over twelve pound,
He broke a rib in his left hand side
    And his intrels fell on the ground,
        And his intrels fell on the ground.

John Henry, O, John Henry,
    His blood is running red,
Fell right down with his hammer to the ground,

Said, "I beat him to the bottom but I'm dead,
    Lawd, beat him to the bottom but I'm dead."

When John Henry was laying there dying,
    The people all by his side,
The very last words they heard him say,
    "Give me a cool drink of water 'fore I die,
        Cool drink of water 'fore I die."

John Henry had a little woman,
    The dress she wore was red,
She went down the track, and she never looked back,
    Going where her man fell dead,
        Going where her man fell dead.

John Henry had a little woman,
    The dress she wore was blue,
De very last words she said to him,
    "John Henry, I'll be true to you,
        John Henry, I'll be true to you."

"Who's gonna shoes yo' little feet,
    Who's gonna glove yo' hand,
Who's gonna kiss yo' pretty, pretty cheek,
    Now you done lost yo' man?
        Now you done lost yo' man?"

"My mammy's gonna shoes my little feet,
    Pappy gonna glove my hand,
My sister's gonna kiss my pretty, pretty cheek,
    Now I done lost my man,
        Now I done lost my man."

They carried him down by the river,
    And buried him in the sand,
And everybody that passed that way,

Said, "There lies that steel-driving man,
   There lies a steel-driving man."

They took John Henry to the river,
   And buried him in the sand,
And every locomotive come a-roaring by,
   Says "There lies that steel-drivin' man,
      Lawd, there lies a *steel*-drivin' man."

Some say he came from Georgia,
   And some from Alabam,
But it's wrote on the rock at the Big Bend Tunnel,
   That he was an East Virginia man,
      Lord, Lord, an East Virginia man.

She Hugged Me and Kissed Me

I see'd her in de Springtime,
I see'd her in de Fall,
I see'd her in de Cotton patch,
A cameing from de Ball.

She hug me, an' she kiss me,
She wrung my han' an' cried.
She said I wus de sweetes' thing
Dat ever lived or died.

She hug me an' she kiss me.
Oh Heaben! De touch o' her han'!
She said I wus de puttiest thing
In de shape o' mortal man.

I told her dat I love her,
Dat my love wus bed-cord strong;
Den I axed her w'en she'd have me,
An' she jes say "Go long!"

Were You There When They Crucified My Lord?

Were you there, when they crucified my Lord?
Were you there, when they crucified my Lord?
Oh, sometimes, it causes me to tremble, tremble, tremble.
Were you there, when they crucified my Lord?

Were you there, when they nailed him to the tree?
Were you there, when they nailed him to the tree?
Oh, sometimes, it causes me to tremble, tremble, tremble.
Were you there, when they nailed him to the tree?

Were you there, when they pierced him in the side?
Were you there, when they pierced him in the side?
Oh, sometimes, it causes me to tremble, tremble, tremble.
Were you there, when they pierced him in the side?

Were you there, when the sun refused to shine?
Were you there, when the sun refused to shine?
Oh, sometimes, it causes me to tremble, tremble, tremble.
Were you there, when the sun refused to shine?

Were you there, when they laid him in the tomb?
Were you there, when they laid him in the tomb?
Oh, sometimes, it causes me to tremble, tremble, tremble.
Were you there, when they laid him in the tomb?

Phillis Wheatley

On Being Brought from Africa to America

'Twas mercy brought me from my *Pagan* land,
Taught my benighted soul to understand
That there's a God, that there's a *Saviour* too:
Once I redemption neither sought nor knew.
Some view our sable race with scornful eye,
"Their colour is a diabolic die."
Remember, *Christians*, *Negroes*, black as *Cain*,
May be refin'd, and join th' angelic train.

An Hymn to the Evening

Soon as the sun forsook the eastern main
The pealing thunder shook the heav'nly plain;
Majestic grandeur! From the zephyr's wing,
Exhales the incense of the blooming spring.
Soft purl the streams, the birds renew their notes,
And through the air their mingled music floats.

   Through all the heav'ns what beauteous dies are spread!
But the west glories in the deepest red:
So may our breasts with ev'ry virtue glow,
The living temples of our God below!

   Fill'd with the praise of him who gives the light;
And draws the sable curtains of the night,
Let placid slumbers sooth each weary mind,
At mourn to wake more heav'nly, more refin'd;
So shall the labours of the day begin
More pure, more guarded from the snares of sin.

   Night's leaden sceptre seals my drousy eyes,
Then cease, my song, till fair *Aurora* rise.

Frances E. W. Harper

The Slave Auction

The sale began—young girls were there,
    Defenceless in their wretchedness,
Whose stifled sobs of deep despair
    Revealed their anguish and distress.

And mothers stood with streaming eyes,
    And saw their dearest children sold;
Unheeded rose their bitter cries,
    While tyrants bartered them for gold.

And woman, with her love and truth—
    For these in sable forms may dwell—
Gaz'd on the husband of her youth,
    With anguish none may paint or tell.

And men, whose sole crime was their hue,
    The impress of their Maker's hand,
And frail and shrinking children, too,
    Were gathered in that mournful band.

Ye who have laid your love to rest,
    And wept above their lifeless clay,
Know not the anguish of that breast,
    Whose lov'd are rudely torn away.

Ye may not know how desolate
    Are bosoms rudely forced to part,

And how a dull and heavy weight
    Will press the life-drops from the heart.

W.E.B. Du Bois

The Song of the Smoke

I am the smoke king,
I am black.
I am swinging in the sky.
I am ringing worlds on high:
I am the thought of the throbbing mills,
I am the soul of the soul toil kills,
I am the ripple of trading rills,

Up I'm curling from the sod,
I am whirling home to God.
I am the smoke king,
I am black.

I am the smoke king,
I am black.
I am wreathing broken hearts,
I am sheathing devils' darts;
Dark inspiration of iron times,
Wedding the toil of toiling climes
Shedding the blood of bloodless crimes,

Down I lower in the blue,
Up I tower toward the true,
I am the smoke king,
I am black.

I am the smoke king,
I am black.

I am darkening with song,
I am hearkening to wrong;
I will be black as blackness can,
The blacker the mantle the mightier the man,
My purpl'ing midnights no day dawn may ban.

I am carving God in night,
I am painting hell in white.
I am the smoke king,
I am black.

I am the smoke king,
I am black.

I am cursing ruddy morn,
I am nursing hearts unborn;
Souls unto me are as mists in the night,
I whiten my blackmen, I beckon my white,
What's the hue of a hide to a man in his might!
Hail, then, grilly, grimy hands,

Sweet Christ, pity toiling lands!
Hail to the smoke king,
Hail to the black!

James Weldon Johnson

O Black and Unknown Bards

O black and unknown bards of long ago,
How came your lips to touch the sacred fire?
How, in your darkness, did you come to know
The power and beauty of the minstrel's lyre?
Who first from midst his bonds lifted his eyes?
Who first from out the still watch, lone and long,
Feeling the ancient faith of prophets rise
Within his dark-kept soul, burst into song?

Heart of what slave poured out such melody
As "Steal away to Jesus"? On its strains
His spirit must have nightly floated free,
Though still about his hands he felt his chains.
Who heard great "Jordan roll"? Whose starward eye
Saw chariot "swing low"? And who was he
That breathed that comforting, melodic sigh,
"Nobody knows de trouble I see"?

What merely living clod, what captive thing,
Could up toward God through all its darkness grope,
And find within its deadened heart to sing
These songs of sorrow, love and faith, and hope?
How did it catch that subtle undertone,
That note in music heard not with the ears?
How sound the elusive reed so seldom blown,
Which stirs the soul or melts the heart to tears.

Let My People Go

And God called Moses from the burning bush,
He called in a still, small voice,
And he said: Moses—Moses —
And Moses listened,
And he answered and said:
Lord, here am I.

And the voice in the bush said: Moses,
Draw not nigh, take off your shoes,
For you're standing on holy ground.
And Moses stopped where he stood,
And Moses took off his shoes,
And Moses looked at the burning bush,
And he heard the voice,
But he saw no man.

Then God again spoke to Moses,
And he spoke in a voice of thunder:
I am the Lord God Almighty,
I am the God of thy fathers,
I am the God of Abraham,
Of Isaac and of Jacob.
And Moses hid his face.

And God said to Moses:
I've seen the awful suffering
Of my people down in Egypt.
I've watched their hard oppressors,
Their overseers and drivers;
The groans of my people have filled my ears
And I can't stand it no longer;
So I'm come down to deliver them
Out of the land of Egypt,

And I will bring them out of that land
Into the land of Canaan;
Therefore, Moses, go down,
Go down into Egypt,
And tell Old Pharaoh
To let my people go.

And Moses said: Lord, who am I
To make a speech before Pharaoh?
For, Lord, you know I'm slow of tongue.
But God said: I will be thy mouth and I will be thy tongue;
Therefore, Moses, go down,
Go down yonder into Egypt land,
And tell Old Pharaoh
To let my people go.

And Moses with his rod in hand
Went down and said to Pharaoh:
Thus saith the Lord God of Israel,
Let my people go.

And Pharaoh looked at Moses,
He stopped still and looked at Moses;
And he said to Moses: Who is this Lord?
I know all the gods of Egypt,
But I know no God of Israel;
So go back, Moses, and tell your God,
I will not let this people go.

Poor Old Pharaoh,
He knows all the knowledge of Egypt,
Yet never knew—
He never knew
The one and the living God.
Poor Old Pharaoh,
He's got all the power of Egypt,

And he's going to try
To test his strength
With the might of the great Jehovah,
With the might of the Lord God of Hosts,
The Lord mighty in battle.
And God, sitting high up in his heaven,
Laughed at poor Old Pharaoh.

And Pharaoh called the overseers,
And Pharaoh called the drivers,
And he said: Put heavier burdens still
On the backs of the Hebrew Children.
Then the people chode with Moses,
And they cried out: Look here, Moses,
You've been to Pharaoh, but look and see
What Pharaoh's done to us now.
And Moses was troubled in mind.

But God said: Go again, Moses,
You and your brother, Aaron,
And say once more to Pharaoh,
Thus saith the Lord God of the Hebrews,
Let my people go.
And Moses and Aaron with their rods in hand
Worked many signs and wonders.
But Pharaoh called for his magic men,
And they worked wonders, too.
So Pharaoh's heart was hardened,
And he would not,
No, he would not
Let God's people go.

And God rained down plagues on Egypt,
Plagues of frogs and lice and locusts,
Plagues of blood and boils and darkness,
And other plagues besides.

But ev'ry time God moved the plague
Old Pharaoh's heart was hardened,
And he would not,
No, he would not
Let God's people go.
And Moses was troubled in mind.

Then the Lord said: Listen, Moses,
The God of Israel will not be mocked,
Just one more witness of my power
I'll give hard-hearted Pharaoh.
This very night about midnight,
I'll pass over Egypt land,
In my righteous wrath will I pass over,
And smite their first-born dead.

And God that night passed over.
And a cry went up out of Egypt.
And Pharaoh rose in the middle of the night
And he sent in a hurry for Moses;
And he said: Go forth from among my people,
You and all the Hebrew Children;
Take your goods and take your flocks,
And get away from the land of Egypt.

And, right then, Moses led them out,
With all their goods and all their flocks;
And God went on before,
A guiding pillar of cloud by day,
And a pillar of fire by night.
And they journeyed on in the wilderness,
And came down to the Red Sea.

In the morning,
Oh, in the morning,
They missed the Hebrew Children.

Four hundred years,
Four hundred years
They'd held them down in Egypt land.
Held them under the driver's lash,
Working without money and without price.
And it might have been Pharaoh's wife that said:
Pharaoh—look what you've done.
You let those Hebrew Children go,
And who's going to serve us now?
Who's going to make our bricks and mortar?
Who's going to plant and plow our corn?
Who's going to get up in the chill of the morning?
And who's going to work in the blazing sun?
Pharaoh, tell me that!

And Pharaoh called his generals,
And the generals called the captains,
And the captains called the soldiers.
And they hitched up all the chariots,
Six hundred chosen chariots of war,
And twenty-four hundred horses.
And the chariots all were full of men,
With swords and shields
And shiny spears
And battle bows and arrows.
And Pharaoh and his army
Pursued the Hebrew Children
To the edge of the Red Sea.

Now, the Children of Israel, looking back,
Saw Pharaoh's army coming.
And the rumble of the chariots was like a thunder storm,
And the whirring of the wheels was like a rushing wind,
And the dust from the horses made a cloud that darked the day,
And the glittering of the spears was like lightnings in the night.

And the Children of Israel all lost faith,
The children of Israel all lost hope;
Deep Red Sea in front of them
And Pharaoh's host behind.
And they mumbled and grumbled among themselves:
Were there no graves in Egypt?
And they wailed aloud to Moses and said:
Slavery in Egypt was better than to come
To die here in this wilderness.

But Moses said:
Stand still! Stand still!
And see the Lord's salvation.
For the Lord God of Israel
Will not forsake his people.
The Lord will break the chariots,
The Lord will break the horsemen,
He'll break great Egypt's sword and shield,
The battle bows and arrows;
This day he'll make proud Pharaoh know
Who is the God of Israel.

And Moses lifted up his rod
Over the Red Sea;
And God with a blast of his nostrils
Blew the waters apart,
And the waves rolled back and stood up in a pile,
And left a path through the middle of the sea
Dry as the sands of the desert.
And the Children of Israel all crossed over
On to the other side.

When Pharaoh saw them crossing dry,
He dashed on in behind them—
Old Pharaoh got about half way cross,
And God unlashed the waters,

And the waves rushed back together,
And Pharaoh and all his army got lost,
And all his host got drownded.
And Moses sang and Miriam danced,
And the people shouted for joy,
And God led the Hebrew Children on
Till they reached the promised land.

Listen!—Listen!
All you sons of Pharaoh.
Who do you think can hold God's people
When the Lord God himself has said,
Let my people go?

Paul Laurence Dunbar

We Wear the Mask

We wear the mask that grins and lies,
It hides our cheeks and shades our eyes,—
This debt we pay to human guile;
With torn and bleeding hearts we smile,
And mouth with myriad subleties.

Why should the world be over-wise,
In counting all our tears and sighs?
Nay, let them only see us, while
    We wear the mask.

We smile, but, O great Christ, our cries
To thee from tortured souls arise.
We sing, but oh the clay is vile
Beneath our feet, and long the mile;
But let the world dream otherwise,
    We wear the mask.

The Debt

This is the debt I pay
Just for one riotous day,
Years of regret and grief,
Sorrow without relief.

Pay it I will to the end—
Until the grave, my friend,
Gives me a true release—
Gives me the clasp of peace.

Slight was the thing I bought,
Small was the debt I thought,
Poor was the loan at best—
God! but the interest!

Little Brown Baby

Little brown baby wif spa'klin' eyes,
    Come to yo' pappy an' set on his knee.
What you been doin', suh—makin' san' pies?
    Look at dat bib—You's ez du'ty ez me.
Look at dat mouf—dat's merlasses, I bet;
    Come hyeah, Maria, an' wipe off his han's.
Bees gwine to ketch you an' eat you up yit,
    Bein' so sticky an' sweet—goodness lan's!

Little brown baby wif spa'klin' eyes,
    Who's pappy's darlin' an' who's pappy's chile?
Who is it all de day nevah once tries
    Fu' to be cross, er once loses dat smile?
Whah did you git dem teef? My, you's a scamp!
    Whah did dat dimple come f'om in yo' chin?
Pappy do' know you—I b'lieves you's a tramp;
    Mammy, dis hyeah's some ol' straggler got in!

Let's th'ow him outen de do' in de san',
    We do' want stragglers a-layin' 'roun' hyeah;
Let's gin him 'way to de big buggah-man;
    I know he's hidin' erroun' hyeah right neah.
Buggah-man, buggah-man, come in de do',
    Hyeah's a bad boy you kin have fu' to eat.
Mammy an' pappy do' want him no mo',
    Swaller him down f'om his haid to his feet!

Dah, now, I t'ought dat you'd hug me up close.
    Go back, ol' buggah, you sha'n't have dis boy.
He ain't no tramp, ner no straggler, of co'se;
    He's pappy's pa'dner an' playmate an' joy.
Come to you' pallet now—go to you' res';
    Wisht you could allus know ease an' cleah skies;

Wisht you could stay jes' a chile on my breas'—
    Little brown baby wif spa'klin eyes!

Ere Sleep Comes Down To Soothe the Weary Eyes

Ere sleep comes down to soothe the weary eyes,
Which all the day with ceaseless care have sought
The magic gold which from the seeker flies;
Ere dreams put on the gown and cap of thought,
And make the waking world a world of lies,—
Of lies most palpable, uncouth, forlorn,
That say life's full of aches and tears and sighs—
Oh, how with more than dreams the soul is torn,
Ere sleep comes down to soothe the weary eyes.

Ere sleep comes down to soothe the weary eyes,
How all the griefs and heartaches we have known
Come up like pois'nous vapors that arise
From some base witch's caldron, when the crone,
To work some potent spell, her magic plies.
The past which held its share of bitter pain,
Whose ghost we prayed that Time might exorcise,
Comes up, is lived and suffered o'er again,
Ere sleep comes down to soothe the weary eyes.

When Malindy Sings

G'way an' quit dat noise, Miss Lucy—
  Put dat music book away;
What's de use to keep on tryin'?
  Ef you practise twell you're gray,
You cain't sta't no notes a-flyin'
  Lak de ones dat rants and rings
From the kitchen to de big woods
  When Malindy sings.

You ain't got de nachel o'gans
  Fu' to make de soun' come right,
You ain't got de tu'ns an' twistin's
  Fu' to make it sweet an' light.
Tell you one thing now, Miss Lucy,
  An' I'm tellin' you fu' true,
When hit comes to raal right singin',
  Tain't no easy thing to do.

Easy 'nough fu' folks to hollah,
  Lookin' at de lines an' dots,
When dey ain't no one kin sence it,
  An' de chune comes in, in spots;
But fu' real melojous music,
  Dat jes' strikes yo' hea't and clings,
Jes' you stan' an listen wif me
  When Malindy sings.

Ain't you nevah hyeahd Malindy?
  Blessed soul, tek up de cross!
Look hyeah, ain't you jokin', honey?
  Well, you don't know whut you los'.
Y'ought to hyeah dat gal a-wa'blin',
  Robins, la'ks, an' all dem things,

Heish dey moufs an' hides dey faces
   When Malindy sings.

Fiddlin' man jes' stop his fiddlin',
   Lay his fiddle on de she'f;
Mockin'-bird quit tryin' to whistle,
   'Cause he jes' so shamed hisse'f.
Folks a-playin' on de banjo
   Draps dey fingahs on de strings—
Bless yo' soul—fu'gits to move 'em,
   When Malindy sings.

She jes' spreads huh mouf and hollahs,
   "Come to Jesus," twell you hyeah
Sinnahs' tremblin' steps and voices,
   Timid-lak a-drawin' neah;
Den she tu'ns to "Rock of Ages,"
   Simply to de cross she clings,
An' you fin' yo' teahs a-drappin'
   When Malindy sings.

Who dat says dat humble praises
   Wif de Master nevah counts?
Heish yo' mouf, I hyeah dat music,
   Ez hit rises up an' mounts—
Floatin' by de hills an' valleys,
   Way above dis buryin' sod,
Ez hit makes its way in glory
   To de very gates of God!

Oh, hit's sweetah dan de music
   Of an edicated band;
An' hit's dearah dan de battle's
   Song o' triumph in de lan'.
It seems holier than evenin'
   When de solemn chu'ch bell rings,

Ez I sit an' ca'mly listen
   While Malindy sings.

Towsah, stop dat ba'kin', hyeah me!
   Mandy, mek dat chile keep still;
Don't you hyeah de echoes callin'
   From de valley to de hill?
Let me listen, I can hyeah it,
   Th'oo de bresh of angel's wings,
Sof' an' sweet, "Swing Low, Sweet Chariot,"
   Ez Malindy sings.

Alice Dunbar Nelson

I Sit and Sew

I sit and sew—a useless task it seems,
My hands grown tired, my head weighed down with dreams—
The panoply of war, the martial tread of men,
Grim-faced, stern-eyed, gazing beyond the ken
Of lesser souls, whose eyes have not seen Death
Nor learned to hold their lives but as a breath—
But—I must sit and sew.

I sit and sew—my heart aches with desire—
That pageant terrible, that fiercely pouring fire
On wasted fields, and writhing grotesque things
Once men. My soul in pity flings
Appealing cries, yearning only to go
There in that holocaust of hell, those fields of woe—
But—I must sit and sew.

The little useless seam, the idle patch;
Why dream I here beneath my homely thatch,
When there they lie in sodden mud and rain,
Pitifully calling me, the quick ones and the slain?
You need me, Christ! It is no roseate dream
That beckons me—this pretty futile seam,
It stifles me—God, must I sit and sew?

Georgia Douglas Johnson

The Heart of a Woman

The heart of a woman goes forth with the dawn,
As a lone bird, soft winging, so restlessly on,
Afar o'er life's turrets and vales does it roam
In the wake of those echoes the heart calls home.

The heart of a woman falls back with the night,
And enters some alien cage in its plight,
And tries to forget it has dreamed of the stars
While it breaks, breaks, breaks on the sheltering bars.

I Want To Die while You Love Me

I want to die while you love me,
While yet you hold me fair,
While laughter lies upon my lips
And lights are in my hair.

I want to die while you love me.
I could not bear to see,
The glory of this perfect day,
Grow dim—or cease to be.

I want to die while you love me.
Oh! who would care to live
Till love has nothing more to ask,
And nothing more to give.

I want to die while you love me,
And bear to that still bed
Your kisses, turbulent, unspent,
To warm me when I'm dead.

Fenton Johnson

Tired

I am tired of work; I am tired of building up somebody else's civilization.
Let us take a rest, M'Lissy Jane.
I will go down to the Last Chance Saloon, drink a gallon or two of gin, shoot a game or two of dice and sleep the rest of the night on one of Mike's barrels.
You will let the old shanty go to rot, the white people's clothes turn to dust, and the Calvary Baptist Church sink to the bottomless pit.
You will spend your days forgetting you married me and your nights hunting the warm gin Mike serves the ladies in the rear of the Last Chance Saloon.
Throw the children into the river; civilization has given us too many. It is better to die than it is to grow up and find out that you are colored.
Pluck the stars out of the heavens. The stars mark our destiny. The stars marked my destiny.
I am tired of civilization.

Claude McKay

The Tropics in New York

Bananas ripe and green, and ginger root,
   Cocoa in pods and alligator pears,
And tangerines and mangoes and grape fruit,
   Fit for the highest prize at parish fairs.

Set in the window, bringing memories
   Of fruit-trees laden by low-singing rills,
And dewy dawns, and mystical blue skies
   In benediction over nun-like hills.

My eyes grew dim, and I could no more gaze;
   A wave of longing through my body swept,
And, hungry for the old familiar ways,
   I turned aside and bowed my head and wept.

In Bondage

I would be wandering in distant fields
Where man, and bird, and beast, live leisurely,
And the old earth is kind, and ever yields
Her goodly gifts to all her children free;
Where life is fairer, lighter, less demanding
And boys and girls have time and space for play
Before they come to years of understanding—
Somewhere I would singing, far away.
For life is greater than the thousand wars
Men wage for it in their insatiate lust,
And will remain like the eternal stars,
When all that shines to-day is drift and dust
But I am bound with you in your mean graves,
O black men, simple slaves of ruthless slaves.

Jean Toomer

Reapers

Black reapers with the sound of steel on stones
Are sharpening scythes. I see them place the hones
In their hip-pockets as a thing that's done,
And start their silent swinging, one by one.
Black horses drive a mower through the weeds,
And there, a field rat, startled, squealing bleeds,
His belly close to ground. I see the blade,
Blood-stained, continue cutting weeds and shade.

Georgia Dusk

The sky, lazily disdaining to pursue
    The setting sun, too indolent to hold
    A lengthened tournament for flashing gold,
Passively darkens for night's barbecue,

A feast of moon and men and barking hounds,
    An orgy for some genius of the South
    With blood-hot eyes and cane-lipped scented mouth,
Surprised in making folk-songs from soul sounds.

The sawmill blows its whistle, buzz-saws stop,
    And silence breaks the bud of knoll and hill,
    Soft settling pollen where ploughed lands fulfill
Their early promise of a bumper crop.

Smoke from the pyramidal sawdust pile
    Curls up, blue ghosts of trees, tarrying low
    Where only chips and stumps are left to show
The solid proof of former domicile.

Meanwhile, the men, with vestiges of pomp,
    Race memories of king and caravan,
    High-priests, an ostrich, and a juju-man,
Go singing through the footpaths of the swamp.

Their voices rise . . . the pine trees are guitars,
    Strumming, pine-needles fall like sheets of rain . . .
    Their voices rise . . . the chorus of the cane
Is carolling a vesper to the stars.

O singers, resinous and soft your songs
    Above the sacred whisper of the pines,
    Give virgin lips to cornfield concubines,
Bring dreams of Christ to dusky cane-lipped throngs.

Song of the Son

Pour, O pour that parting soul in song,
O pour it in the saw-dust glow of night,
Into the velvet pine-smoke air to-night,
And let the valley carry it along,
And let the valley carry it along.

O land and soil, red soil and sweet-gum tree,
So scant of grass, so profligate of pines,
Now just before an epoch's sun declines
Thy son, in time, I have returned to thee,
Thy son, I have in time returned to thee.

In time, although the sun is setting on
A song-lit race of slaves, it has not set;
Though late, O soil, it is not too late yet
To catch thy plaintive soul, leaving, soon gone,
Leaving, to catch thy plaintive soul soon gone.

O Negro slaves, dark purple ripened plums,
Squeezed, and bursting in the pine-wood air,
Passing, before they strip the old tree bare
One plum was saved for me, one seed becomes

An everlasting song, a singing tree,
Carolling softly souls of slavery,
What they were, and what they are to me,
Carolling softly souls of slavery.

Brown River, Smile

It is a new America,
To be spiritualized by each new American.

Lift, lift, thou waking forces!
Let us feel the energy of animals,
The energy of rumps and bull-bent heads
Crashing the barrier to man.
It must spiral on!
A million million men, or twelve men,
Must crash the barrier to the next higher form.

>   Beyond plants are animals,
>   Beyond animals is man.
>   Beyond man is the universe.
>
>   The Big Light,
>   Let the Big Light in!

O thou, Radiant Incorporeal,
The I of earth and of mankind, hurl
Down these seaboards, across this continent,
The thousand-rayed discus of thy mind,
And above our walking limbs unfurl
Spirit-torsos of exquisite strength!

The Mississippi, sister of the Ganges,
Main artery of earth in the western world,
Is waiting to become
In the spirit of America, a sacred river.
Whoever lifts the Mississippi
Lifts himself and all America;
Whoever lifts himself
Makes that great brown river smile.

The blood of earth and the blood of man
Course swifter and rejoice when we spiritualize.

The old gods, led by an inverted Christ,
A shaved Moses, a blanched Lemur,
And a moulting thunderbird,
Withdrew into the distance and soon died,
Their dust and seed falling down
To fertilize the five regions of America.

We are waiting for a new God.

The old peoples—
The great European races sent wave after wave
That washed the forests, the earth's rich loam,
Grew towns with the seeds of giant cities,
Made roads, laid golden rails,
Sang once of its swift achievement,
And died congested in machinery.
They say that near the end
It was a world of crying men and hard women,
A city of goddam and Jehovah
Baptized in industry
Without benefit of saints,
Of dear defectives
Winnowing their likenesses from weathered rock
Sold by national organizations of undertakers.

Someone said:
    Suffering is impossible
    On cement sidewalks, in skyscrapers,
    In motorcars;
    Steel cannot suffer—
    We die unconsciously
    Because possessed by a nonhuman symbol.

Another cried:
    It is because of thee, O Life,
    That the first prayer ends in the last curse.

Another sang:
    Late minstrels of the restless earth,
    No muteness can be granted thee,
    Lift thy laughing energies
    To that white point which is a star.

The great African races sent a single wave
And singing riplets to sorrow in red fields,
Sing a swan song, to break rocks
And immortalize a hiding water boy.

    I'm leaving the shining ground, brothers,
    I sing because I ache,
    I go because I must,
    Brothers, I am leaving the shining ground;
    Don't ask me where,
    I'll meet you there,
    I'm leaving the shining ground.

The great red race was here.
In a land of flaming earth and torrent-rains,
Of red sea-plains and majestic mesas,
At sunset from a purple hill
The Gods came down;
They serpentined into pueblo,
And a white-robed priest
Danced with them five days and nights;
But pueblo, priest, and Shalicos
Sank into the sacred earth
To fertilize the five regions of America.

Hi-ye, hi-yo, hi-yo
Hi-ye, hi-yo, hi-yo,
A lone eagle feather,
An untamed Navaho,
The ghosts of buffaloes,
Hi-ye, hi-yo, hi-yo,
Hi-ye, hi-yo, hi-yo.

We are waiting for a new people.

O thou, Radiant Incorporeal,
The I of earth and of mankind, hurl
Down these seaboards, across this continent,
The thousand-rayed discus of thy mind,
And above our walking limbs unfurl
Spirit-torsos of exquisite strength!

The east coast is masculine,
The west coast is feminine,
The middle region is the child—
Forces of reconciling
And generator of symbols.

>   Thou, great fields, waving thy growths across the world,
>   Couldest thou find the seed which started thee?
>   Can you remember the first great hand to sow?
>   Have you memory of His intention?
>   Great plains, and thou, mountains,
>   And thou, stately trees, and thou,
>   America, sleeping and producing with the seasons,
>   No clever dealer can divide,
>   No machine can undermine thee.

The prairie's sweep is flat infinity,
The city's rise is perpendicular to farthest star,
I stand where the two directions intersect,

At Michigan Avenue and Walton Place,
Parallel to my countrymen,
Right-angled to the universe.

It is a new America,
To be spiritualized by each new American.

Melvin B. Tolson

Dark Symphony

I
Allegro Moderato

Black Crispus Attucks taught
                      Us how to die
Before white Patrick Henry's bugle breath
Uttered the vertical
                      Transmitting cry:
"Yea, give me liberty or give me death."

Waifs of the auction block,
                      Men black and strong
The juggernauts of despotism withstood,
Loin-girt with faith that worms
                      Equate the wrong
And dust is purged to create brotherhood.

No Banquo's ghost can rise
                      Against us now,
Aver we hobnailed Man beneath the brute,
Squeezed down the thorns of greed
                      On Labor's brow,
Garroted lands and carted off the loot.

II
Lento Grave

The centuries-old pathos in our voices
Saddens the great white world,
And the wizardry of our dusky rhythms
Conjures up shadow-shapes of ante-bellum years:

Black slaves singing *One More River to Cross*
In the torture tombs of slave-ships,
Black slaves singing *Steal Away to Jesus*
In jungle swamps,
Black slaves singing *The Crucifixion*
In slave-pens at midnight,
Black slaves singing *Swing Low, Sweet Chariot*
In cabins of death,
Black slaves singing *Go Down, Moses*
In the canebrakes of the Southern Pharaohs.

III
Andante Sostenuto

They tell us to forget
The Golgotha we tread . . .
We who are scourged with hate,
A price upon our head.
They who have shackled us
Require of us a song,
They who have wasted us
Bid us condone the wrong.

They tell us to forget
Democracy is spurned.
They tell us to forget
The Bill of Rights is burned.
Three hundred years we slaved,

We slave and suffer yet:
Though flesh and bone rebel,
They tell us to forget!

Oh, how can we forget
Our human rights denied?
Oh, how can we forget
Our manhood crucified?
When Justice is profaned
And plea with curse is met,
When Freedom's gates are barred,
Oh, how can we forget?

IV
Tempo Primo

The New Negro strides upon the continent
In seven-league boots . . .
The New Negro
Who sprang from the vigor-stout loins
Of Nat Turner, gallows-martyr for Freedom,
Of Joseph Cinquez, Black Moses of the Amistad Mutiny,
Of Frederick Douglass, oracle of the Catholic Man,
Of Sojourner Truth, eye and ear of Lincoln's legions,
Of Harriet Tubman, Saint Bernard of the Underground Railroad.

The New Negro
Breaks the icons of his detractors,
Wipes out the conspiracy of silence,
Speaks to *his* America:

"My history-moulding ancestors
Planted the first crops of wheat on these shores,
Built ships to conquer the seven seas,
Erected the Cotton Empire,
Flung railroads across a hemisphere,

Disemboweled the earth's iron and coal,
Tunneled the mountains and bridged rivers,
Harvested the grain and hewed forests,
Sentineled the Thirteen Colonies,
Unfurled Old Glory at the North Pole,
Fought a hundred battles for the Republic."

The New Negro:
His giant hands fling murals upon high chambers,
His drama teaches a world to laugh and weep,
His music leads continents captive,
His voice thunders the Brotherhood of Labor,
His science creates seven wonders,
His Republic of Letters challenges the Negro-baiters.

The New Negro,
Hard-muscled, Fascist-hating, Democracy-ensouled,
Strides in seven-league boots
Along the Highway of Today
Toward the Promised Land of Tomorrow!

V
Larghetto

None in the Land can say
To us black men Today:
You send the tractors on their bloody path,
And create Okies for *The Grapes of Wrath*.
You breed the slum that breeds a *Native Son*
To damn the good earth Pilgrim Fathers won.

None in the Land can say
To us black men Today:
You dupe the poor with rags-to-riches tales,
And leave the workers empty dinner pails.

You stuff the ballot box, and honest men
Are muzzled by your demagogic din.

None in the Land can say
To us black men Today:
You smash stock markets with your coined blitzkriegs,
And make a hundred million guinea pigs.
You counterfeit our Christianity,
And bring contempt upon Democracy.

None in the Land can say
To us black men Today:
You prowl when citizens are fast asleep,
And hatch Fifth Column plots to blast the deep
Foundations of the State and leave the Land
A vast Sahara with a Fascist brand.

VI
Tempo di Marcia

Out of abysses of Illiteracy,
Through labyrinths of Lies,
Across waste lands of Disease . . .
We advance!

Out of dead-ends of Poverty,
Through wildernesses of Superstition,
Across barricades of Jim Crowism . . .
We advance!

With the Peoples of the World . . .
We advance!

African China

I

A connoisseur of pearl
necklace phrases,
Wu Shang disdains
his laundry, lazes
among his bric-a-brac
metaphysical;
and yet dark customers,
on Harlem's rack
quizzical,
sweat and pack
the forked caldera of
his Stygian shop:
some worship God,
and some Be-Bop.

Wu Shang discovers
the diademed word to be,
on the sly,
a masterkey
to Harlem pocketbooks,
outjockeyed by
policy
and brimstone
theology
alone!

II

As bust and hips
her corset burst,
An Amazonian fantasy,

A Witness of Jehovah
by job and husband curst,
lumbers in.
A yellow mummy in a mummery
a tip-toe,
Wu Shang unsheathes a grin,
and then, his fingers sleeved,
gulps an ugh and eats his crow,
disarmed by ugliness disbelieved!

At last he takes his wits
from balls of moth,
salaams. "Dear Lady, I, for you,
wear goats' sackcloth
to mark this hour and place;
cursed be the shadow of delay
that for a trice conceals a trace
of beauty in thy face!"

Her jug of anger emptied, now he sighs:
"Her kind cannot play euchre.
The master trick belongs to him
who holds the joker."
His mind's eye sees a black hand drop
a red white poker.

III

The gingered gigolo,
vexed by the harrow of a date
and vanity torn,
goddamns the yellow sage,
four million yellow born,
and yellow fate!

The gigolo
a wayward bronco
seen but unheard,
Wu Shang applies the curb-bit word:
"Wise lovers know
that in their lottery success
belongs to him who plays a woman
with titbits of a guess."

The sweet man's sportive whack
Paralyzes Wu Shang's back.
"Say, Yellah Boy, I call yo' stuff
the hottest dope in town!
That red hot mama'll never know
she got her daddy down."

IV

Sometimes the living dead
stalk in and sue for grace,
the tragic uncommon
in the comic commonplace,
the evil that the good
begets in love's embrace,
a Harlem melodrama
like that in Big John's face

as Wu Shang peers at him
and cudgels a theorem.
The sage says in a voice ilang-ilang,
"Do you direct the weathercock?"
And then his lash, a rackarock,
descends with a bang,
"Show me the man who has not thrown
a boomerang!"

. . . words, no longer pearls,
but drops of Gilead's balm.
Later, later, Wu Shang remarks,
"Siroccos mar the toughest palm."
The bigger thing, as always, goes unsaid:
the look behind the door of Big John's eyes,
awareness of the steps of *Is*,
the freedom of the wise.

V

When Dixie Dixon breaks a leg
on arctic Lenox Avenue
and Wu Shang homes her, pays her fees,
old kismet knots the two
unraveled destinies.
The unperfumed
wag foot, forefinger, head;
and belly laughter waifs ghost rats
foxed by the smell of meat and bread;
and black walls blab, "Good Gawd,
China and Africa gits wed!"

VI

Wu Shang, whom nothing sears,
says Dixie is a dusky passion flower
unsoiled by envious years.
And Dixie says
her Wu Shang is a Mandarin
with seven times seven ways of love,
her very own oasis in
the desert
of Harlem men.

In dignity, Wu Shang and Dixie walk
the gauntlet, Lenox Avenue;
their son has Wu Shang's cast
and Dixie's hue.

The dusky children roll
their oyster eyes
at Wu Shang, Junior, flash
a premature surmise,
as if afraid:
in accents Carolina
on the streets they never made,
the dusky children tease,
"African China!"

Frank Horne

Walk

I am trying
to learn to walk again . . .
all tensed and trembling
I try so hard, so hard . . .

Not like the headlong patter
of new and anxious feet
or the vigorous flailing of the water
by young swimmers
beating
a new element
into submission . . .
It is more like
a timorous Lazarus
commanded
to take up the bed
on which he died . . .

I know I will walk again
into your healing
outstretched arms
in answer
to your tender command . . .

I have been lost
and fallen
in the dark underbrush

but I will arise
and walk
and find the path
at your soft command.

Notes Found Near a Suicide

TO ALL OF YOU

My little stone
Sinks quickly
Into the bosom of this deep, dark pool
Of oblivion . . .
I have troubled its breast but little
Yet those far shores
That knew me not
Will feel the fleeting, furtive kiss
Of my tiny concentric ripples . . .

TO MOTHER

I came
In the blinding sweep
Of ecstatic pain,
I go
In the throbbing pulse
Of aching space—
In the eons between
I piled upon you
Pain on pain
Ache on ache
And yet as I go
I shall know
That you will grieve
And want me back . . .

TO CATALINA

Love thy piano, Oh girl,
It will give you back

Note for note
The harmonies of your soul.
It will sing back to you
The high songs of your heart.
It will give
As well as take . . .

TO TELIE

You have made my voice
A rippling laugh
But my heart
A crying thing . . .
'Tis better thus:
A fleeting kiss
And then,
The dark . . .

TO "CHICK"

Oh Achilles of the moleskins
And the gridiron
Do not wonder
Nor doubt that this is I
That lies so calmly here—
This is the same exultant beast
That so joyously
Ran the ball with you
In those far-flung days of abandon.
You remember how recklessly
We revelled in the heat and the dust
And the swirl of conflict?
You remember they called us
The Terrible Two?
And you remember
After we had battered our heads

And our bodies
Against the stonewall of their defense,—
You remember the signal I would call
And how you would look at me
In faith and admiration
And say "Let's go," . . .
How the lines would clash
And strain,
And how I would slip through
Fighting and squirming
Over the line
To victory.
You remember, Chick? . . .
When you gaze at me here
Let that same light
Of faith and admiration
Shine in your eyes
For I have battered the stark stonewall
Before me . . .
I have kept faith with you
And now
I have called my signal,
Found my opening
And slipped through
Fighting and squirming
Over the line
To victory. . . .

TO WANDA

To you, so far away
So cold and aloof,
To you, who knew me so well,
This is my last Grand Gesture
This is my last Great Effect
And as I go winging

Through the black doors of eternity
Is that thin sound I hear
Your applause? . . .

TO JAMES

Do you remember
How you won
That last race . . . ?
How you flung your body
At the start . . .
How your spikes
Ripped the cinders
In the stretch . . .
How you catapulted
Through the tape . . .
Do you remember . . . ?
Don't you think
I lurched with you
Out of those starting holes . . . ?
Don't you think
My sinews tightened
At those first
Few strides . . .
And when you flew into the stretch
Was not all my thrill
Of a thousand races
In your blood . . . ?
At your final drive
Through the finish line
Did not my shout
Tell of the
Triumphant ecstasy
Of victory . . . ?
Live
As I have taught you

To run, Boy—
It's a short dash
Dig your starting holes
Deep and firm
Lurch out of them
Into the straightaway
With all the power
That is in you
Look straight ahead
To the finish line
Think only of the goal
Run straight
Run high
Run hard
Save nothing
And finish
With an ecstatic burst
That carries you
Hurtling
Through the tape
To victory . . .

TO THE POETS

Why do poets
Like to die
And sing raptures to the grave?

They seem to think
That bitter dirt
Turns sweet between the teeth.

I have lived
And yelled hosannas
At the climbing stars

I have lived
And drunk deep
The deceptive wine of life . . .

And now, tipsy and reeling
From its dregs
I die . . .

Oh, let the poets sing
Raptures to the grave.

TO HENRY

I do not know
How I shall look
When I lie down here
But I really should be smiling
Mischievously . . .
You and I have studied
Together
The knowledge of the ages
And lived the life of Science
Matching discovery for discovery—
And yet
In a trice
With a small explosion
Of this little machine
In my hand
I shall know
All
That Aristotle, Newton, Lavoisier, and Galileo
Could not determine
In their entire
Lifetimes . . .
And the joke of it is,
Henry,

That I have
Beat you to it . . .

TO ONE WHO CALLED ME "NIGGER"

You are Power
And send steel ships hurtling
From shore to shore . . .

You are Vision
And cast your sight through eons of space
From world to world . . .

You are Brain
And throw your voice endlessly
From ear to ear . . .

You are Soul
And falter at the yawning chasm
From White to Black . . .

TO CAROLINE

Your piano
Is the better instrument . . .
Yesterday
Your fingers
So precisely
Touched the cold keys—
A nice string
Of orderly sounds
A proper melody . . .
Tonight
Your hands
So wantonly
Caressed my tingling skin—

A mad whirl
Of cacophony,
A wild chanting . . .
Your piano
Is the better instrument.

TO ALFRED

I have grown tired of you
And your wife
Sitting there
With your children,
Little bits of you
Running about your feet
And you two so calm
And cold together . . .
It is really better
To lie here
Insensate
Than to see new life
Creep upon you
Calm and cold
Sitting there . . .

TO YOU

All my life
They have told me
That You
Would save my Soul
That only
By kneeling in Your House
And eating of Your Body
And drinking of Your Blood
Could I be born again . . .
And yet

One night
In the tall black shadow
Of a windy pine
I offered up
The Sacrifice of Body
Upon the altar
Of her breast . . .
You
Who were conceived
Without ecstasy
Or pain
Can you understand
That I knelt last night
In Your House
And ate of Your Body
And drank of Your Blood.
. . . and thought only of her?

Sterling Brown

Strange Legacies

One thing you left with us, Jack Johnson.
One thing before they got you.

You used to stand there like a man,
Taking punishment
With a golden, spacious grin;
Confident.
Inviting big Jim Jeffries, who was boring in:
"Heah ah is, big boy; yuh sees whah Ise at.
Come on in. . . . "

Thanks, Jack, for that.

John Henry, with your hammer;
John Henry, with your steel driver's pride,
You taught us that a man could go down like a man,
Sticking to your hammer till you died.
Sticking to your hammer till you died.

Brother,
When, beneath the burning sun
The sweat poured down and the breath came thick,
And the loaded hammer swung like a ton
And the heart grew sick;
You had what we need now, John Henry.
Help us get it.

So if we go down
Have to go down
We go like you, brother,
'Nachal' men. . . .

Old nameless couple in Red River Bottom,
Who have seen floods gutting out your best loam,
And the boll weevil chase you
Out of your hard-earned home,
Have seen the drought parch your green fields,
And the cholera stretch your porkers out dead;
Have seen year after year
The commissary always a little in the lead;
Even you said
That which we need
Now in our time of fear,—

Routed your own deep misery and dread,
Muttering, beneath an unfriendly sky,
"Guess we'll give it one mo' try.
Guess we'll give it one mo' try."

Strong Men

The strong men keep coming on.—*Sandburg*

They dragged you from the homeland,
They chained you in coffles,
They huddled you spoon-fashion in filthy hatches,
They sold you to give a few gentlemen ease.

They broke you in like oxen,
They scourged you,
They branded you,
They made your women breeders,
They swelled your numbers with bastards. . . . .
They taught you the religion they disgraced.
You sang:
> Keep a-inchin' along
> Lak a po' inch worm . . .

You sang:
> By and bye
> I'm gonna lay down this heaby load . . .

You sang:
> Walk togedder, chillen,
> Dontcha git weary . . .
>> The strong men keep a-comin' on
>> The strong men get stronger.

They point with pride to the roads you built for them,
They ride in comfort over the rails you laid for them.
They put hammers in your hands
And said—Drive so much before sundown.
You sang:
> Ain't no hammah
> In dis lan'

>   Strikes lak mine, bebby,
>   Strikes lak mine.
They cooped you in their kitchens,
They penned you in their factories,
They gave you the jobs that they were too good for,
They tried to guarantee happiness to themselves
By shunting dirt and misery to you.
You sang:
>   Me an' muh baby gonna shine, shine
>   Me an' muh baby gonna shine.
>   The strong men keep a-comin' on
>   The strong men git stronger . . .

They bought off some of your leaders
You stumbled, as blind men will . . .
They coaxed you, unwontedly soft-voiced . . .
You followed a way.
Then laughed as usual.
They heard the laugh and wondered;
Uncomfortable;
Unadmitting a deeper terror . . .
>   The strong men keep a-comin' on
>   Gittin' stronger . . .

What, from the slums
Where they have hemmed you,
What, from the tiny huts
They could not keep from you—
What reaches them
Making them ill at ease, fearful?
Today they shout prohibition at you
"Thou shalt not this"
"Thou shalt not that"
"Reserved for whites only"
You laugh.

One thing they cannot prohibit—

> The strong men . . . coming on
> The strong men gittin' stronger.
> Strong men . . .
> Stronger . . .

Arna Bontemps

Close Your Eyes!

Go through the gates with closed eyes.
Stand erect and let your black face front the west.
Drop the axe and leave the timber where it lies;
A woodman on the hill must have his rest.

Go where leaves are lying brown and wet.
Forget her warm arms and her breast who mothered you,
And every face you ever loved forget.
Close your eyes; walk bravely through.

Southern Mansion

Poplars are standing there still as death
and ghosts of dead men
meet their ladies walking
two by two beneath the shade
and standing on the marble steps.

There is a sound of music echoing
through the open door
and in the field there is
another sound tinkling in the cotton:
chains of bondmen dragging on the ground.

The years go back with an iron clank,
a hand is on the gate,
a dry leaf trembles on the wall.
Ghosts are walking.
They have broken roses down
and poplars stand there still as death.

The Return

I

Once more, listening to the wind and rain,
Once more, you and I, and above the hurting sound
Of these comes back the throbbing of remembered rain,
Treasured rain falling on dark ground.
Once more, huddling birds upon the leaves
And summer trembling on a withered vine.
And once more, returning out of pain,
The friendly ghost that was your love and mine.

II

Darkness brings the jungle to our room:
The throb of rain is the throb of muffled drums.
Darkness hangs our room with pendulums
Of vine and in the gathering gloom
Our walls recede into a denseness of
Surrounding trees. This is a night of love
Retained from those lost nights our fathers slept
In huts; this is a night that must not die.
Let us keep the dance of rain our fathers kept
And tread our dreams beneath the jungle sky.

III

And now the downpour ceases.
Let us go back once more upon the glimmering leaves
And as the throbbing of the drums increases
Shake the grass and dripping boughs of trees.
A dry wind stirs the palm; the old tree grieves.

Time has charged the years: the old days have returned.

Let us dance by metal waters burned
With gold of moon, let us dance
With naked feet beneath the young spice trees.
What was that light, that radiance
On your face?—something I saw when first
You passed beneath the jungle tapestries?

A moment we pause to quench our thirst
Kneeling at the water's edge, the gleam
Upon your face is plain: you have wanted this.
Let us go back and search the tangled dream
And as the muffled drum-beats throb and miss
Remember again how early darkness comes
To dreams and silence to the drums.

IV

Let us go back into the dusk again,
Slow and sad-like following the track
Of blowing leaves and cool white rain
Into the old gray dream, let us go back.
Our walls close about us we lie and listen
To the noise of the street, the storm and the driven birds.
A question shapes your lips, your eyes glisten
Retaining tears, but there are no more words.

A Black Man Talks of Reaping

I have sown beside all waters in my day.
I planted deep, within my heart the fear
That wind or fowl would take the grain away.
I planted safe against this stark, lean year.

I scattered seed enough to plant the land
In rows from Canada to Mexico
But for my reaping only what the hand
Can hold at once is all that I can show.

Yet what I sowed and what the orchard yields
My brother's sons are gathering stalk and root,
Small wonder then my children glean in fields
They have not sown, and feed on bitter fruit.

Nocturne at Bethesda

I thought I saw an angel flying low,
I thought I saw the flicker of a wing
Above the mulberry trees; but not again.
Bethesda sleeps. That ancient pool that healed
A host of bearded Jews does not awake.

This pool that once the angels troubled does not move
No angel stirs it now, no Saviour comes
With healing in His hands to raise the sick
And bid the lame man leap upon the ground.

The golden days are gone. Why do we wait
So long upon the marble steps, blood
Falling from our open wounds? and why
Do our black faces search the empty sky?
Is there something we have forgotten? some precious thing
We have lost, wandering in strange lands?

There was a day, I remember now,
I beat my breast and cried, "Wash me God,
Wash me with a wave of wind upon
The barley; O quiet One, draw near, draw near!
Walk upon the hills with lovely feet
And in the waterfall stand and speak.

"Dip white hands in the lily pool and mourn
Upon the harps still hanging in the trees
Near Babylon along the river's edge,
But oh, remember me, I pray, before
The summer goes and rose leaves lose their red."

The old terror takes my heart, the fear
Of quiet waters and of faint twilights.

There will be better days when I am gone
And healing pools where I cannot be healed.
Fragrant stars will gleam forever and ever
Above the place where I lie desolate.

Yet I hope, still I long to live.
And if there can be returning after death
I shall come back. But it will not be here;
If you want me you must search for me
Beneath the palms of Africa. Or if
I am not there then you may call to me
Across the shining dunes, perhaps I shall
Be following a desert caravan.

I may pass through centuries of death
With quiet eyes, but I'll remember still
A jungle tree with burning scarlet birds.
There is something I have forgotten, some precious thing.
I shall be seeking ornaments of ivory,
I shall be dying for a jungle fruit.

    You do not hear, Bethesda.
O still green water in a stagnant pool!
Love abandoned you and me alike.
There was a day you held a rich full moon
Upon your heart and listened to the words
Of men now dead and saw the angels fly.
There is a simple story on your face;
Years have wrinkled you. I know, Bethesda!
You are sad. It is the same with me.

Langston Hughes

Jazzonia

Oh, silver tree!
Oh, shining rivers of the soul!

In a Harlem cabaret
Six long-headed jazzers play.
A dancing girl whose eyes are bold
Lifts high a dress of silken gold.

Oh, singing tree!
Oh, shining rivers of the soul!

Were Eve's eyes
In the first garden
Just a bit too bold?
Was Cleopatra gorgeous
In a gown of gold?

Oh, shining tree!
Oh, silver rivers of the soul!

In a whirling cabaret
Six long-headed jazzers play.

The Negro Speaks of Rivers

To W.E.B. Du Bois

I've known rivers:
I've known rivers ancient as the world and older than
    the flow of human blood in human veins.

My soul has grown deep like the rivers.

I bathed in the Euphrates when dawns were young.
I built my hut near the Congo and it lulled me to sleep.
I looked upon the Nile and raised the pyramids above it.
I heard the singing of the Mississippi when Abe
    Lincoln went down to New Orleans, and I've seen
    its muddy bosom turn all golden in the sunset.

I've known rivers:
Ancient, dusky rivers.

My soul has grown deep like the rivers.

I, Too, Sing America

I, too, sing America.

I am the darker brother.
They send me to eat in the kitchen
When company comes,
But I laugh,
And eat well,
And grow strong.

Tomorrow,
I'll be at the table
When company comes.
Nobody'll dare
Say to me,
"Eat in the kitchen,"
Then.

Besides,
They'll see how beautiful I am
And be ashamed—

I, too, am America.

Dream Deferred

What happens to a dream deferred?

    Does it dry up
    like a raisin in the sun?
    Or fester like a sore—
    And then run?
    Does it stink like rotten meat?
    Or crust and sugar over—
    like a syrupy sweet?

    Maybe it just sags
    like a heavy load.

    Or does it explode?

Freedom

Freedom will not come
Today, this year
    Nor ever
Through compromise and fear.

I have as much right
As the other fellow has
    To stand
On my two feet
And own the land.

I tire so of hearing people say,
Let things take their course.
Tomorrow is another day.
I do not need my freedom when I'm dead.
I cannot live on tomorrow's bread.
    Freedom
    Is a strong seed
    Planted
    In a great need.
    I live here, too.
    I want freedom
    Just as you.

Countee Cullen

Yet Do I Marvel

I doubt not God is good, well-meaning, kind,
And did He stoop to quibble could tell why
The little buried mole continues blind,
Why flesh that mirrors Him must some day die,
Make plain the reason tortured Tantalus
Is baited by the fickle fruit, declare
If merely brute caprice dooms Sisyphus
To struggle up a never-ending stair.
Inscrutable His ways are, and immune
To catechism by a mind too strewn
With petty cares to slightly understand
What awful brain compels His awful hand.
Yet do I marvel at this curious thing:
To make a poet black, and bid him sing!

Robert Hayden

O Daedalus, Fly Away Home

Drifting night in the Georgia pines,
coonskin drum and jubilee banjo.
   Pretty Malinda, dance with me.

Night is juba, night is conjo.
   Pretty Malinda, dance with me.

Night is an African juju man
weaving a wish and a weariness together
   to make two wings.

   O fly away home fly away

Do you remember Africa?

   O cleave the air fly away home

My gran, he flew back to Africa,
just spread his arms and
   flew away home.

Drifting night in the windy pines;
night is a laughing, night is a longing.
   Pretty Malinda, come to me.

Night is a mourning juju man
weaving a wish and a weariness together
 to make two wings.

O fly away home fly away

Homage to the Empress of the Blues

Because there was a man somewhere in a candystripe silk shirt,
gracile and dangerous as a jaguar and because a woman moaned
for him in sixty-watt gloom and mourned him Faithless Love
Twotiming Love Oh Love Oh Careless Aggravating Love,

> She came out on the stage in yards of pearls, emerging like
> a favorite scenic view, flashed her golden smile and sang.

Because grey laths began somewhere to show from underneath
torn hurdygurdy lithographs of dollfaced heaven;
and because there were those who feared alarming fists of snow
on the door and those who feared the riot-squad of statistics,

> She came out on the stage in ostrich feathers, beaded satin,
> and shone that smile on us and sang.

Frederick Douglass

When it is finally ours, this freedom, this liberty, this beautiful
and terrible thing, needful to man as air,
usable as earth; when it belongs at last to all,
when it is truly instinct, brain matter, diastole, systole,
reflex action; when it is finally won; when it is more
than the gaudy mumbo jumbo of politicians:
this man, this Douglass, this former slave, this Negro
beaten to his knees, exiled, visioning a world
where none is lonely, none hunted, alien,
this man, superb in love and logic, this man
shall be remembered. Oh, not with statues' rhetoric,
not with legends and poems and wreaths of bronze alone,
but with the lives grown out of his life, the lives
fleshing his dream of the beautiful, needful thing.

In the Mourning Time

As the gook woman howls
for her boy in the smouldering,
as the expendable Clean-Cut Boys
From Decent American Homes
are slashing off enemy ears for keepsakes;

as the victories are tallied up
with flag-draped coffins, plastic bodybags,
what can my sorrow anger pity say
but this, this:

We must not be frightened nor cajoled
into accepting evil as deliverance from evil.
We must go on struggling to be human,
though monsters of abstraction
police and threaten us.

Reclaim now, now renew the vision of
a human world where godliness
is possible and man
is neither gook nigger honkey wop nor kike

but man

           permitted to be man.

The Night-Blooming Cereus

    And so for nights
we waited, hoping to see
the heavy bud
    break into flower.

    On its neck-like tube
hooking down from the edge
of the leaf-branch
    nearly to the floor,

    the bud packed
tight with its miracle swayed
stiffly on breaths
    of air, moved

    as though impelled
by stirrings within itself.
It repelled as much
    as it fascinated me

    sometimes—snake,
eyeless bird head,
beak that would gape
    with grotesque life-squawk.

    But you, my dear,
conceded less to the bizarre
than to the imminence
    of bloom. Yet we agreed

    we ought
to celebrate the blossom,

paint ourselves, dance
    in honor of

    archaic mysteries
when it appeared. Meanwhile
we waited, aware
    of rigorous design.

    Backster's
polygraph, I thought,
would have shown
    (as clearly as it had

    a philodendron's
fear) tribal sentience
in the cactus, focused
    energy of will.

    That belling of
tropic perfume—that
signaling
    not meant for us;

    the darkness
cloyed with summoning
fragrance. We dropped
    trivial tasks

    and marveling
beheld at last the achieved
flower. Its moonlight
    petals were

    still unfold-
ing, the spike fringe of the outer

perianth recessing
    as we watched.

    Lunar presence,
foredoomed, already dying,
it charged the room
    with plangency

    older than human
cries, ancient as prayers
invoking Osiris, Krishna,
    Tezcátlipóca.

    We spoke
in whispers when
we spoke
    at all . . .

Middle Passage

I

Jesús, Estrella, Esperanza, Mercy:

    Sails flashing to the wind like weapons,
    sharks following the moans the fever and the dying;
    horror the corposant and compass rose.

Middle Passage:
    voyage through death
        to life upon these shores.

    "10 April 1800—
    Blacks rebellious. Crew uneasy. Our linguist says
    their moaning is a prayer for death,
    ours and their own. Some try to starve themselves.
    Lost three this morning leaped with crazy laughter
    to the waiting sharks, sang as they went under."

Desire, Adventure, Tartar, Ann:

    Standing to America, bringing home
    black gold, black ivory, black seed.

      Deep in the festering hold thy father lies,
      of his bones New England pews are made,
      those are altar lights that were his eyes.

Jesus Saviour Pilot Me
Over Life's Tempestuous Sea

We pray that Thou wilt grant, O Lord,
safe passage to our vessels bringing
heathen souls unto Thy chastening.

Jesus Saviour

> "8 bells. I cannot sleep, for I am sick
> with fear, but writing eases fear a little
> since still my eyes can see these words take shape
> upon the page & so I write, as one
> would turn to exorcism. 4 days scudding,
> but now the sea is calm again. Misfortune
> follows in our wake like sharks (our grinning
> tutelary gods). Which one of us
> has killed an albatross? A plague among
> our blacks—Ophthalmia: blindness—& we
> have jettisoned the blind to no avail.
> It spreads, the terrifying sickness spreads.
> Its claws have scratched sight from the Capt.'s eyes
> & there is blindness in the fo'c'sle
> & we must sail 3 weeks before we come
> to port."

> *What port awaits us, Davy Jones'*
> *or home? I've heard of slavers drifting, drifting,*
> *playthings of wind and storm and chance, their crews*
> *gone blind, the jungle hatred*
> *crawling up on deck.*

Thou Who Walked On Galilee

> "Deponent further sayeth *The Bella J*
> left the Guinea Coast
> with cargo of five hundred blacks and odd
> for the barracoons of Florida:

"That there was hardly room 'tween-decks for half
the sweltering cattle stowed spoon-fashion there;
that some went mad of thirst and tore their flesh
and sucked the blood:

"That Crew and Captain lusted with the comeliest
of the savage girls kept naked in the cabins;
that there was one they called The Guinea Rose
and they cast lots and fought to lie with her:

"That when the Bo's'n piped all hands, the flames
spreading from starboard already were beyond
control, the negroes howling and their chains
entangled with the flames:

"That the burning blacks could not be reached,
that the Crew abandoned ship,
leaving their shrieking negresses behind,
that the Captain perished drunken with the wenches:

"Further Deponent sayeth not."

Pilot Oh Pilot Me

II

Aye, lad, and I have seen those factories,
Gambia, Rio Pongo, Calabar;
have watched the artful mongos baiting traps
of war wherein the victor and the vanquished

Were caught as prizes for our barracoons.
Have seen the nigger kings whose vanity
and greed turned wild black hides of Fellatah,
Mandingo, Ibo, Kru to gold for us.

And there was one—King Anthracite we named him—
fetish face beneath French parasols
of brass and orange velvet, impudent mouth
whose cups were carven skulls of enemies:

He'd honor us with drum and feast and conjo
and palm-oil-glistening wenches deft in love,
and for tin crowns that shone with paste,
red calico and German-silver trinkets

Would have the drums talk war and send
his warriors to burn the sleeping villages
and kill the sick and old and lead the young
in coffles to our factories.

Twenty years a trader, twenty years,
for there was wealth aplenty to be harvested
from those black fields, and I'd be trading still
but for the fevers melting down my bones.

III

Shuttles in the rocking loom of history,
the dark ships move, the dark ships move,
their bright ironical names
like jests of kindness on a murderer's mouth;
plough through thrashing glister toward
fata morgana's lucent melting shore,
weave toward New World littorals that are
mirage and myth and actual shore.

Voyage through death,
                      voyage whose chartings are unlove.

A charnel stench, effluvium of living death
spreads outward from the hold,

where the living and the dead, the horribly dying,
lie interlocked, lie foul with blood and excrement.

> *Deep in the festering hold thy father lies,*
> *the corpse of mercy rots with him,*
> *rats eat love's rotten gelid eyes.*
>
> *But, oh, the living look at you*
> *with human eyes whose suffering accuses you,*
> *whose hatred reaches through the swill of dark*
> *to strike you like a leper's claw.*
>
> *You cannot stare that hatred down*
> *or chain the fear that stalks the watches*
> *and breathes on you its fetid scorching breath;*
> *cannot kill the deep immortal human wish,*
> *the timeless will.*

"But for the storm that flung up barriers
of wind and wave, *The Amistad,* señores,
would have reached the port of Príncipe in two,
three days at most; but for the storm we should
have been prepared for what befell.
Swift as the puma's leap it came. There was
that interval of moonless calm filled only
with the water's and the rigging's usual sounds,
then sudden movement, blows and snarling cries
and they had fallen on us with machete
and marlinspike. It was as though the very
air, the night itself were striking us.
Exhausted by the rigors of the storm,
we were no match for them. Our men went down
before the murderous Africans. Our loyal
Celestino ran from below with gun
and lantern and I saw, before the cane-
knife's wounding flash, Cinquez,

that surly brute who calls himself a prince,
directing, urging on the ghastly work.
He hacked the poor mulatto down, and then
he turned on me. The decks were slippery
when daylight finally came. It sickens me
to think of what I saw, of how these apes
threw overboard the butchered bodies of
our men, true Christians all, like so much jetsam.
Enough, enough. The rest is quickly told:
Cinquez was forced to spare the two of us
you see to steer the ship to Africa,
and we like phantoms doomed to rove the sea
voyaged east by day and west by night,
deceiving them, hoping for rescue,
prisoners on our own vessel, till
at length we drifted to the shores of this
your land, America, where we were freed
from our unspeakable misery. Now we
demand, good sirs, the extradition of
Cinquez and his accomplices to La
Havana. And it distresses us to know
there are so many here who seem inclined
to justify the mutiny of these blacks.
We find it paradoxical indeed
that you whose wealth, whose tree of liberty
are rooted in the labor of your slaves
should suffer the august John Quincy Adams
to speak with so much passion of the right
of chattel slaves to kill their lawful masters
and with his Roman rhetoric weave a hero's
garland for Cinquez. I tell you that
we are determined to return to Cuba
with our slaves and there see justice done. Cinquez—
or let us say 'the Prince'—Cinquez shall die."

The deep immortal human wish,
the timeless will:

    Cinquez its deathless primaveral image,
    life that transfigures many lives.

Voyage through death
                     to life upon these shores.

Those Winter Sundays

Sundays too my father got up early
and put his clothes on in the blueblack cold,
then with cracked hands that ached
from labor in the weekday weather made
banked fires blaze. No one ever thanked him.

I'd wake and hear the cold splintering, breaking.
When the rooms were warm, he'd call,
and slowly I would rise and dress,
fearing the chronic angers of that house,

Speaking indifferently to him,
who had driven out the cold
and polished my good shoes as well.
What did I know, what did I know
of love's austere and lonely offices?

Runagate Runagate

I

Runs falls rises stumbles on from darkness into darkness
and the darkness thicketed with shapes of terror
and the hunters pursuing and the hounds pursuing
and the night cold and the night long and the river
to cross and the jack-muh-lanterns beckoning beckoning
and blackness ahead and when shall I reach that somewhere
morning and keep on going and never turn back and keep on
    going

    Runagate
        Runagate
            Runagate

Many thousands rise and go
many thousands crossing over

                O mythic North
                O star-shaped yonder Bible city

Some go weeping and some rejoicing
some in coffins and some in carriages
some in silks and some in shackles

    Rise and go or fare you well

No more auction block for me
no more driver's lash for me

    If you see my Pompey, 30 yrs of age,
    new breeches, plain stockings, negro shoes;
    if you see my Anna, likely young mulatto

branded E on the right cheek, R on the left,
catch them if you can and notify subscriber.
Catch them if you can, but it won't be easy.
They'll dart underground when you try to catch them,
plunge into quicksand, whirlpools, mazes,
turn into scorpions when you try to catch them.

And before I'll be a slave
I'll be buried in my grave

    North star and bonanza gold
    I'm bound for the freedom, freedom-bound
    and oh Susyanna don't you cry for me

        Runagate

            Runagate

II

Rises from their anguish and their power,

        Harriet Tubman,

        woman of earth, whipscarred,
        a summoning, a shining

    Mean to be free

And this was the way of it, brethren brethren,
way we journeyed from Can't to Can.
Moon so bright and no place to hide,
the cry up and the patterollers riding,
hound dogs belling in bladed air.
And fear starts a-murbling, Never make it,
we'll never make it. *Hush that now,*

and she's turned upon us, levelled pistol
glinting in the moonlight:
Dead folks can't jaybird-talk, she says;
you keep on going now or die, she says.

Wanted   Harriet Tubman   alias The General
alias Moses   Stealer of Slaves

In league with Garrison   Alcott   Emerson
Garrett   Douglass   Thoreau   John Brown

Armed and known to be Dangerous

Wanted   Reward   Dead or Alive

    Tell me, Ezekiel, oh tell me do you see
    mailed Jehovah coming to deliver me?

Hoot-owl calling in the ghosted air,
five times calling to the hants in the air.
Shadow of a face in the scary leaves,
shadow of a voice in the talking leaves:

    Come ride-a my train

Oh that train, ghost-story train
through swamp and savanna movering movering,
over trestles of dew, through caves of the wish,
Midnight Special on a sabre track movering movering,
first stop Mercy and the last Hellelujah.

    Come ride-a my train

        Mean mean mean to be free.

The Prisoners

Steel doors—guillotine gates—
of the doorless house closed massively.
We were locked in with loss.

Guards frisked us, marked our wrists,
then let us into the drab Rec Hall—
splotched green walls, high windows barred—

where the dispossessed awaited us.
Hands intimate with knife and pistol,
hands that had cruelly grasped and throttled

clasped ours in welcome. I sensed the plea
of men denied: Believe us human
like yourselves, who but for Grace. . . .

We shared reprieving Hidden Words
revealed by the Godlike imprisoned
One, whose crime was truth.

And I read poems I hoped were true.
It's like you been there, brother, been there,
the scarred young lifer said.

Dudley Randall

Legacy: My South

What desperate nightmare rapts me to this land
Lit by a bloody moon, red on the hills,
Red in the valleys? Why am I compelled
To tread again where buried feet have trod,
To shed my tears where blood and tears have flowed?
Compulsion of the blood and of the moon
Transports me. I was molded from this clay
My blood must ransom all the blood shed here,
My tears redeem the tears. Cripples and monsters
Are here. My flesh must make them whole and hale.
I am the sacrifice.

                See where the halt
Attempt again and again to cross a line
Their minds have drawn, but fear snatches them back
Though health and joy wait on the other side.
And there another locks himself in a room
And throws away the key. A ragged scarecrow
Cackles an antique lay, and cries himself
Lord of the world. A naked plowman falls
Famished upon the plow, and overhead
A lean bird circles.

The Southern Road

There the black river, boundary to hell.
And here the iron bridge, the ancient car,
And grim conductor, who with surly yell
Forbids white soldiers where the black ones are.
And I re-live the enforced avatar
Of desperate journey to a dark abode
Made by my sires before another war;
And I set forth upon the southern road.

To a land where shadowed songs like flowers swell
And where the earth is scarlet as a scar
Friezed by the bleeding lash that fell (O fell)
Upon my fathers' flesh. O far, far, far
And deep my blood has drenched it. None can bar
My birthright to the loveliness bestowed
Upon this country haughty as a star.
And I set forth upon the southern road.

This darkness and these mountains loom a spell
Of peak-roofed town where yearning steeples soar
And the holy holy chanting of a bell
Shakes human incense on the throbbing air
Where bonfires blaze and quivering bodies char.
Whose is the hair that crisped, and fiercely glowed?
I know it; and my entrails melt like tar
And I set forth upon the southern road.

O fertile hillsides where my fathers are,
From which my griefs like troubled streams have flowed,
I have to love you, though they sweep me far.
And I set forth upon the southern road.

Gwendolyn Brooks

When You Have Forgotten Sunday: The Love Story

——And when you have forgotten the bright bedclothes
    on a Wednesday and a Saturday,
And most especially when you have forgotten Sunday—
When you have forgotten Sunday halves in bed,
Or me sitting on the front-room radiator in the limping
    afternoon
Looking off down the long street
To nowhere,
Hugged by my plain old wrapper of no-expectation
And nothing-I-have-to-do and I'm-happy-why?
And if-Monday-never-had-to-come—
When you have forgotten that, I say,
And how you swore, if somebody beeped the bell,
And how my heart played hopscotch if the telephone
    rang;
And how we finally went in to Sunday dinner,
That is to say, went across the front room floor to the
    ink-spotted table in the southwest corner
To Sunday dinner, which was always chicken and
    noodles
Or chicken and rice
And salad and rye bread and tea
And chocolate chip cookies—
I say, when you have forgotten that,
When you have forgotten my little presentiment
That the war would be over before they got to you;

And how we finally undressed and whipped out the
    light and flowed into bed,
And lay loose-limbed for a moment in the week-end
Bright bedclothes,
Then gently folded into each other—
When you have, I say, forgotten all that,
Then you may tell,
Then I may believe
You have forgotten me well.

The Bean Eaters

They eat beans mostly, this old yellow pair.
Dinner is a casual affair.
Plain chipware on a plain and creaking wood,
Tin flatware.

Two who are Mostly Good.
Two who have lived their day,
But keep on putting on their clothes
And putting things away.

And remembering . . .
Remembering, with twinklings and twinges,
As they lean over the beans in their rented back room that
    is full of beads and receipts and dolls and cloths,
    tobacco crumbs, vases and fringes.

The Sermon on the Warpland

"The fact that we are black is our ultimate reality."
—*Ron Karenga*

And several strengths from drowsiness campaigned
but spoke in Single Sermon on the warpland.

And went about the warpland saying No.
"My people, black and black, revile the River.
Say that the River turns, and turn the River.

Say that our Something in doublepod contains
seeds for the coming hell and health together.
Prepare to meet
(sisters, brothers) the brash and terrible weather;
the pains;
the bruising; the collapse of bestials, idols.
But then oh then!—the stuffing of the hulls!
the seasoning of the perilously sweet!
the health! the heralding of the clear obscure!

Build now your Church, my brothers, sisters. Build
never with brick nor Corten nor with granite.
Build with lithe love. With love like lion-eyes.
With love like morningrise.
With love like black, our black—
luminously indiscreet;
complete; continuous."

The Second Sermon on the Warpland

For Walter Bradford

1.

This is the urgency: Live!
and have your blooming in the noise of the whirlwind.

2.

Salve salvage in the spin.
Endorse the splendor splashes;
Stylize the flawed utility;
prop a malign or failing light—
but know the whirlwind is our commonwealth.
Not the easy man, who rides above them all,
not the jumbo brigand,
not the pet birds of poets, that sweetest sonnet,
shall straddle the whirlwind.
Nevertheless, live.

3.

All about are the cold places,
all about are the pushmen and jeopardy, theft—
all about are the stormers and scramblers but
what must our Season be, which starts from Fear?
Live and go out.
Define and
medicate the whirlwind.

4.

The time

cracks into furious flower. Lifts its face
all unashamed. And sways in wicked grace.
Whose half-black hands assemble oranges
is tom-tom hearted
(goes in bearing oranges and boom).
And there are bells for orphans—
and red and shriek and sheen.
A garbageman is dignified
as any diplomat
Big Bessie's feet hurt like nobody's business,
but she stands—bigly—under the unruly scrutiny, stands in the
    wild weed.

In the wild weed
she is a citizen,
and is a moment of highest quality; admirable.

It is lonesome, yes. For we are the last of the loud.
Nevertheless, live.

Conduct your blooming in the noise and whip of the whirlwind.

Life for My Child Is Simple and Is Good

Life for my child is simple, and is good.
He knows his wish. Yes, but that is not all.
Because I know mine too.
And we both want joy of undeep and unabiding things,
Like kicking over a chair or throwing blocks out of a window
Or tipping over an icebox pan
Or snatching down curtains or fingering an electric outlet
Or a journey or a friend or an illegal kiss.
No. There is more to it than that.
It is that he has never been afraid.
Rather, he reaches out and lo the chair falls with a beautiful
    crash,
And the blocks fall, down on the people's heads,
And the water comes slooshing sloppily out across the floor.
And so forth.
Not that success, for him, is sure, infallible.
But never has he been afraid to reach.
His lesions are legion.
But reaching is his rule.

Naomi Long Madgett

Mortality

This is the surest death
Of all the deaths I know.
The one that halts the breath,
The one that falls with snow
Are nothing but a peace
Before the second zone,
For Aprils never cease
To resurrect their own,
And in my very veins
Flows blood as old as Eve.
The smallest cell contains
Its privileged reprieve.
But vultures recognize
This single mortal thing
And watch with hungry eyes
When hope starts staggering.

Midway

I've come this far to freedom and I won't turn back.
I'm climbing to the highway from my old dirt track.
    I'm coming and I'm going
    And I'm stretching and I'm growing
And I'll reap what I've been sowing or my skin's not black.

I've prayed and slaved and waited and I've sung my song.
You've bled me and you've starved me but I've still grown
    strong.
    You've lashed me and you've treed me
    And you've everything but freed me
But in time you'll know you need me and it won't be long.

I've seen the daylight breaking high above the bough.
I've found my destination and I've made my vow;
    So whether you abhor me
    Or deride me or ignore me,
Mighty mountains loom before me and I won't stop now.

Simple
(For Langston Hughes)

He sits at the bar in the Alhambra
looking down Seventh Avenue
through the open door.
He wants to talk, but the stool beside
        him
is empty
and no one he knows is coming down the
        street.

      Hey man, I got problems—ya know?
      Could ya let me have another fin
      jes' till nex' Friday, huh?
      I gotta get in to change my clothes
      but my lan'lady's bolted the door
          again.
      If Joyce don't get to go to that
          show
      again tonight, man,
      my name really be mud!

The landlady's bolted the door for good
this time
and he will never go home.

Joyce will tap her toe impatiently
        awhile
and then go out alone.
through a long, long night
he will stare at his empty beer glass
and the vacant stool
and soon he will wonder what it was
he wanted to say.

Black Woman

My hair is springy like the forest grasses
That cushion the feet of squirrels—
Crinkled and blown in a south breeze
Like the small leaves of native bushes.

My black eyes are coals burning
Like a low, full, jungle moon
Through the darkness of being.
In a clear pool I see my face,
Know my knowing.

My hands move pianissimo
Over the music of the night:
Gentle birds fluttering through leaves and grasses
They have not always loved,
Nesting, finding home.

Where are my lovers?
Where are my tall, my lovely princes
Dancing in slow grace
Toward knowledge of my beauty?
Where
Are my beautiful
Black men?

Derek Walcott

Upstate

A knife blade of cold air keeps prying
the bus window open. The spring country
won't be shut out. The door to the john
keeps banging. There're a few of us:
a stale-drunk or stoned woman in torn jeans,
a Spanish-American salesman, and, ahead,
a black woman folded in an overcoat.
Emptiness makes a companionable aura
through the upstate villages—repetitive,
but crucial in their little differences
of fields, wide yards with washing, old machinery—where people
     live
with the highway's patience and flat certainty.

Sometimes I feel sometimes
the Muse is leaving, the Muse is leaving America.
Her tired face is tired of iron fields,
its hollows sing the mines of Appalachia,
she is a chalk-thin miner's wife with knobbled elbows,
her neck tendons taut as banjo strings,
she who was once a freckled palomino with a girl's mane
galloping blue pastures plinkety-plunkety,
staring down at a tree-stunned summer lake,
when all the corny calendars were true.
The departure comes over me in smoke
from the far factories.

But were the willows lyres, the fanned-out pollard willows
with clear translation of water into song,
were the starlings as heartbroken as nightingales,
whose sorrow piles the looming thunderhead
over the Catskills, what would be their theme?
The spring hills are sun-freckled, the chaste white barns flash
through screening trees the vigor of her dream,
like a white plank bridge over a quarreling brook.
Clear images! Direct as your daughters
in the way their clear look returns your stare,
unarguable and fatal—
no, it is more sensual.
I am falling in love with America.

I must put the cold small pebbles from the spring
upon my tongue to learn her language,
to talk like birch or aspen confidently.
I will knock at the widowed door
of one of these villages
where she will admit me like a broad meadow,
like a blue space between mountains,
and holding her arms at the broken elbows
brush the dank hair from a forehead
as warm as bread or as a homecoming.

Etheridge Knight

The Idea of Ancestry

1

Taped to the wall of my cell are 47 pictures: 47 black
faces: my father, mother, grandmothers (1 dead), grand
fathers (both dead), brothers, sisters, uncles, aunts,
cousins (1st & 2nd), nieces, and nephews. They stare
across the space at me sprawling on my bunk. I know
their dark eyes, they know mine. I know their style,
they know mine. I am all of them, they are all of me;
they are farmers, I am a thief, I am me, they are thee.

I have at one time or another been in love with my mother,
1 grandmother, 2 sisters, 2 aunts (1 went to the asylum),
and 5 cousins. I am now in love with a 7 yr old niece
(she sends me letters written in large block print, and
her picture is the only one that smiles at me).

I have the same name as 1 grandfather, 3 cousins, 3 nephews,
and 1 uncle. The uncle disappeared when he was 15, just took
off and caught a freight (they say). He's discussed each year
when the family has a reunion, he causes uneasiness in
the clan, he is an empty space. My father's mother, who is 93
and who keeps the Family Bible with everybody's birth dates
(and death dates) in it, always mentions him. There is no
place in her Bible for "whereabouts unknown."

2

Each Fall the graves of my grandfathers call me, the brown
hills and red gullies of mississippi send out their electric
messages, galvanizing my genes. Last yr/like a salmon quitting
the cold ocean—leaping and bucking up his birthstream/I
hitchhiked my way from L.A. with 16 caps in my pocket and a
monkey on my back. and I almost kicked it with the kinfolks.
I walked barefooted in my grandmother's backyard/I smelled the
  old
land and the woods/I sipped cornwhiskey from fruit jars with the
  men/
I flirted with the women/I had a ball till the caps ran out
and my habit came down. That night I looked at my grandmother
and split/my guts were screaming for junk/but I was almost
contented/I had almost caught up with me.
(The next day in Memphis I cracked a croaker's crib for a fix.)

This yr there is a gray stone wall damming my stream, and when
the falling leaves stir my genes, I pace my cell or flop on my
  bunk
and stare at 47 black faces across the space. I am all of them,
they are all of me, I am me, they are thee, and I have no sons
to float in the space between.

He Sees Through Stone

He sees through stone
he has the secret
eyes this old black one
who under prison skies
sits pressed by the sun
against the western wall
his pipe between purple gums

the years fall
like overripe plums
bursting red flesh
on the dark earth

his time is not my time
but I have known him
in a time gone

he led me trembling cold
into the dark forest
taught me the secret rites
to take a woman
to be true to my brothers
to make my spear drink
the blood
of my enemies

now black cats circle him
flash white teeth
snarl at the air
mashing green grass beneath
shining muscles
ears peeling his words
he smiles

he knows
the hunt   the enemy
he has the secret eyes
he sees through stone
His forehead is red
and sacrosanct and
smooth as time and
love for you

It Was a Funky Deal

It was a funky deal.
The only thing real was red,
Red blood around his red, red beard.

It was a funky deal.

In the beginning was the word,
And in the end the deed.
Judas did it to Jesus
For the same Herd. Same reason.
You made them mad, Malcolm. Same reason.

It was a funky deal.

You rocked too many boats, man.
Pulled too many coats, man.
Saw through the jive.
You reached the wild guys
Like me. You and Bird. (And that
Lil LeRoi cat.)

It was a funky deal.

Leroi Jones

The Insidious Dr. Fu Manchu

If I think myself
strong, then I am
not true to the misery
in my life. The uncertainty.
(of what I am saying, who
I have chose to become, the
very air pressing my skin
held gently away, this woman
and the one I taste continually
in my nebular pallet tongue face
mouth feet, standing in piles
of numbers, hills, lovers.
                        If

I think myself ugly
& go to the mirror, smiling,
at the inaccuracy, or Now
the rain pounds dead grass
in the stone yard, I think
how very wise I am. How very
very wise.

The Liar

What I thought was love
in me, I find a thousand instances
as fear. (Of the tree's shadow
winding around the chair, a distant music
of frozen birds rattling
in the cold.
               Where ever I go to claim
my flesh, there are entrances
of spirit. And even its comforts
are hideous uses I strain
to understand.
              Though I am a man
who is loud
on the birth
of his ways. Publicly redefining
each change in my soul, as if I had predicted
them,
      and profited, biblically, even tho
      their chanting weight,
                     erased familiarity
                     from my face.
                            A question I think,
an answer; whatever sits
counting the minutes
till you die.

        When they say, "It is Roi
        who is dead?" I wonder
        who will they mean?

Cold Term

All the things. The objects.
Cold freeze of the park, while
passing. People there. White inside
outside on horses trotting ignorantly
There is so much pain for our blackness
so much beauty there, if we think to what
our beautiful selves would make
of the world, steaming turning blackouts
over cold georgia, the spirits hover
waiting for the world to arrive at ecstasy.
Why cant we love each other and be beautiful?
Why do the beautiful corner each other and spit
poison? Why do the beautiful not hangout together
and learn to do away with evil? Why are the beautiful
not living together and feeling each other's trials?
Why are the beautiful not walking with their arms around
each other laughing softly at the soft laughter of black beauty?
Why are the beautiful dreading each other, and hiding from
each other? Why are the beautiful sick and divided
like myself?

Jitterbugs

The imperfection of the world
is a burden, if you know it, think
about it, at all. Look up in the sky
wishing you were free, placed so terribly
in time, mind out among new stars, working
propositions, and not this planet where you
cant go anywhere without an awareness of the hurt
the white man has put on the people. Any people. You
cant escape, there's no where to go. They have made
this star unsafe, and this age, primitive, though yr mind
is somewhere else, your ass aint.

A Poem Some People Will Have To Understand

Dull unwashed windows of eyes
and buildings of industry. What
industry do I practice? A slick
colored boy, 12 miles from his
home. I practice no industry.
I am no longer a credit
to my race. I read a little,
scratch against silence slow spring
afternoons.
        I had thought, before, some years ago
that I'd come to the end of my life.
        Watercolor ego. Without the preciseness
a violent man could propose.
        But the wheel, and the wheels,
wont let us alone. All the fantasy
        and justice, and dry charcoal winters
All the pitifully intelligent citizens
        I've forced myself to love.

        We have awaited the coming of a natural
        phenomenon. Mystics and romantics,
            knowledgeable
        workers
        of the land.

        But none has come.
        (Repeat)
            but none has come.

Will the machinegunners please step forward?

Young Soul

First, feel, then feel, then
read, or read, then feel, then
fall, or stand, where you
already are. Think
of your self, and the other
selves . . . think
of your parents, your mothers
and sisters, your bentslick
father, then feel, or
fall, on your knees
if nothing else will move you,

                                        then read
                                        and look deeply
                                        into all matters
                                        come close to you
                                        city boys—
                                        country men

                                        Make some muscle
                                        in your head, but
                                        use the muscle
                                        in yr heart

Audre Lorde

Coal

I
is the total black, being spoken
from the earth's inside.
There are many kinds of open
how a diamond comes into a knot of flame
how sound comes into a words, coloured
by who pays what for speaking.

Some words are open like a diamond
on glass windows
singing out within the crash of sun
Then there are words like stapled wagers
in a perforated book—buy and sign and tear apart—
and come whatever wills all chances
the stub remains
an ill-pulled tooth with a ragged edge.
Some words live in my throat
breeding like adders. Others know sun
seeking like gypsies over my tongue
to explode through my lips
like young sparrows bursting from shell.
Some words
bedevil me.

Love is a word, another kind of open.
As the diamond comes into a knot of flame

I am Black because I come from the earth's inside
Now take my word for jewel in the open light.

Another says mother
I am holding your place.
Do you know me better than I knew him
or myself?
Am I his daughter or girlfriend
am I your child or your rival
you wish to be gone from his bed?
Here is your granddaughter mother
give me your blessing before I sleep
what other secrets
do you have to tell me
how do I learn to love her
as you have loved me?

Summer Oracle

Without expectation
there is no end
to the shocks of morning
or even a small summer.

Now the image is fire
blackening the vague lines
into defiance across the city.
The image is fire
sun warming us in a cold country
barren of symbols for love.

Now I have forsaken order
and imagine you into fire
untouchable in a magician's coat
covered with signs of destruction and birth
sewn with griffins and arrows and hammers
And gold sixes stitched into your hem
your fingers draw fire
but still the old warlocks shun you
for no gourds ring in your sack
no spells bring forth peace
and I am still fruitless and hungry
this summer
the peaches are flinty and juiceless
and cry sour worms.

The image is fire
flaming over you burning off excess
like the blaze planters start
To burn off bagasse from the canefields
After a harvest.

The image is fire
the high sign that rules our summer
I smell it in the charred breezes blowing over
your body
close
hard
essential
under its cloak of lies.

The Woman Thing

The hunters are back from beating the winter's face
in search of a challenge or task
in search of food
making fresh tracks for their children's hunger
they do not watch the sun
they cannot wear its heat for a sign
of triumph or freedom.
The hunters are treading heavily homeward
through snow that is marked
with their own bloody footprints.
Emptyhanded the hunters return
snow-maddened, sustained by their rages.

In the night after food they may seek
young girls for their amusement. But now
the hunters are coming
and the unbaked girls flee from their angers.

All this day I have craved
food for my child's hunger.
Emptyhanded the hunters come shouting
injustices drip from their mouths
like stale snow melted in sunlight.

Meanwhile the womanthing my mother taught me
bakes off its covering of snow
like a rising blackening sun.

Bob Kaufman

To My Son Parker, Asleep in the Next Room

On ochre walls in ice-formed caves shaggy Neanderthals
   marked their place in time.
On germinal trees in equatorial stands embryonic giants
   carved beginnings.
On Tasmanian flatlands mud-clothed first men hacked rock,
   still soft.
On Melanesian mountain peaks barked heads were reared
   in pride and beauty.
On steamy Java's cooling lava stooped humans raised stones
   to altar height.
On newborn China's plain mythless sons of Han acquired
   peaked gods with teak faces.
On holy India's sacred soil future gods carved worshipped
   reflections.
On Coptic Ethiopia's pimple rock pyramid builders tore
   volcanoes from earth.
On death-loving Egypt's godly sands living sacrifices carved
   naked power.
On Sumeria's cliffs speechless artists gouged messages
   to men yet uncreated.
On glorious Assyria's earthen dens art priests chipped
   figures of awe and hidden dimensions.
On splendored Peru's gold-stained body filigreed temples
   were torn from severed hands.
On perfect Greece's bloody sites marble stirred
   under hands of men.

On degenerate Rome's trembling sod imitators sculpted lies
    into beauty.
On slave Europe's prostrate form chained souls shaped free
    men.
On wild America's green torso original men painted
    glacial languages.
On cold Arctica's snowy surface leathery men raised totems
    in frozen air.
On this shore, you are all men, before, forever, eternally
    free in all things.
On this shore, we shall raise our monuments of stones,
        of wood, of mud, of color, of labor, of belief, of being,
        of life, of love, of self, of man expressed
        in self-determined compliance, or willful revolt,
        secure in this avowed truth, that no man is our master,
        nor can any ever be, at any time in time to come.

Sonia Sanchez

Right On: Wite America

3.

this country might have
been a pio
       neer land
once.
    but.   there ain't
no mo
      indians   blowing
custer's mind
         with a different
image of america.
            this country
might have
       needed shoot/
outs/daily/
     once.
           but there ain't
no mo real/wite/   all american
             bad/guys.
just.
   u & me.
        blk/and un/armed.
this country might have
been a pion
      eer land.   once.
              and it still is.

        check out
                    the falling
        gun/shells   on our blk/tomorrows.

Last Poem I'm Gonna Write about Us

some
      times i dream bout
              u & me
                     runnen down
a street laughen.
          me no older
          u no younger
              than we be.
& we finalee catch
          each other.
              laugh.   tooouch
in the nite.
      some
         times
            i turn a corner
of my mind
      & u be there
           loooooking
                at me.
& smilen.
     yo/far/away/smile.
           & i moooove
to u.
   & the day is not any day. & yes ter day
is looonNNg
      goooNNe. & we just be. Some
times i be steady dreamen bout u
            cuz i waaannNt
neeeeEEeeD u so
      baaaaAdDD.
    with u no younger &
    me no older
        than we be.

Poem at Thirty

it is midnight
no magical bewitching
hour for me
i know only that
i am here waiting
remembering that
once as a child
i walked two
miles in my sleep.

Poem No. 4

i am here in
my usual place
nothing is turned

on. even i cannot
turn from this
quiet unfolding

my skin. O i am
marked with
this nite's welts

wooing my hands
until they creep
as slowly as a

child's ache, i
touch my pulse.
tell me O pulse

is my breath
out of tune?
i am not a

face of my
own choosing.
still. i am.

i am. and see
my soul elaborate
with furs.

Pennsylvania Dutch Country

this is power
ful country
my man. the
redyellow trees
blast your eyes
until they close
in self defense.
                pennsylvania dutch
country would turn
you on   would make
you run with the leaves until your
limbs cut them
down.
                powerful man
                that you are.
                What a joy
to love you here
                on a hill
where massive trees
would change colors
as we changed each
others' skins.
                man. this
                country
would be more powerful
with you
                and
                me. . . .

Lucille Clifton

Good Times

My Daddy has paid the rent
and the insurance man is gone
and the lights is back on
and my uncle Brud has hit
for one dollar straight
and they is good times
good times
good times

My mama has made bread
and Grampaw has come
and everybody is drunk
and dancing in the kitchen
and singing in the kitchen
oh these is good times
good times
good times

oh children think about the
good times

June Jordan

All the World Moved

All the world moved next to me strange
I grew on my knees
in hats and taffeta trusting
the holy water to run
like grief from a brownstone
cradling.

Blessing a fear of the anywhere
face too pale to be family
my eyes wore ribbons
for Christ on the subway
as weekly as holiness
in Harlem.

God knew no East no West no South
no Skin nothing I learned like
traditions of sin but later
life began and strangely
I survived His innocence
without my own.

For Christopher

Tonight
   the machinery of shadow
      moves into the light

He is lying there
   not a true invalid
      not dying

Now his face looks blue
     but all of that small body
       will more than do
          as life.

The lady radiologist
     regardless how and where
        she turns the knob
will never know
     the plenty of pain
         growing

parts to arm
   a man inside the boy

practically asleep

Roman Poem Number Thirteen
For Eddie

Only our hearts will argue hard
against the small lights letting in the news
and who can choose between the worst possibility
and the last
between the winners of the wars against the breathing
and the last
war everyone will lose
and who can choose between the dry gas
domination of the future
and the past
between the consequences of the killers
and the past
of all the killing? There
is no choice in these.
Your voice
breaks very close to me my love.

About the Reunion

"I am rarely vindictive but
this summer I have taken great
pleasure in killing mosquitoes"

He says that to me
It is quite dark where we sit
and difficult to see

or tells me of work he will do
films of no end no beginning
and pours more wine
or takes another cigarette

And I know that is probably true
of his life of our love not to begin
not to end not be ugly or fine

But there is this history of once
when his hands and the length of his legs
came suddenly
to claim me all
bone and all flesh forcing away
the wall and the image of the wall
in one
fast meeting of amazement

And that was another year and somewhere
else

Here we talk outside
or do not talk

almost asleep in separated

wood chairs as hard as the time
between us
and
I admit
you are not as tall as the trees around me
your eyes are not as open as surprising
as the sea

but I watch for your words any changing
of your head
from a deadspot in the darkness
to a face

and finally you move

"I have to get in touch with
some other people"
you say
after so much silence

and I do not move

and
you leave.

Clarence Major

Waiting in the Children's Hospital
(1957)

I reflect on this desperate note
while waiting in the children's hospital.
The desperate cry my son left
cold as ice in his closed eyes after poison.

Benches of blood. This is a wooden tragedy.

Joyce & I walked home under the huge night
thru a grand rain sweep and
around midnight I scribble a letter to my sister,
who is dying five minutes at a time:
       You are the flower of confusion
       coming up in the morning
       of my love and
       going tightly shut in the afternoon of
       anger. Anger & bitterness.
               I look forward to your resurrection.

I get up tonight and walk naked
through the wet weeds. The moon is smiling
and it has no teeth.

I walk home less, the huge night in me.

I remember a trillion stars in the Lexington night
above all shadows ahead of me but

I cannot remember the feeling
of a little girl's kiss.   Do you remember?

I remember I walked to town with a blind
man beside me singing or was he humming.
That same summer of a trillion grasshoppers. And
I loved him through & beyond his blackness.
His woman in a shack beside the highway
with four grandbabies in a wooden bed;
fanning summer flies from the syrup on their lips.

But the blood is white this summer.

Roasted ears. The hog season & my uncle
was a good shot. The blood is red this summer
redder than redbirds.

I felt that I had to go along in silence
with the heart of a monk, face flat to the earth
arms outstretched. & when I got up
I walked close to walls.
I moved with my head low and my hands hidden
like a starved Christian, meaning
to do this forever.

Form

I am the form that comes to nightwatch.
I am the form that comes with a gun.
I organize your thoughts, tell you the *words*.
I make up things. I hear voices.
Feel fire. The radio is a voice.
The lamp is a light.
The hotplate is a fire.
My leather coat is an animal in pain.
The sounds of bricks falling on the roof
    are sleeping pills.
I am the form that sleeps through the noise.
I organize the dream at the end of the word.
I start the fire at the root of things.
The words keep revealing themselves as our bodies.
Your body is like mine: reaching out
    to close itself around sleep.
My nightwatch turns to daydreaming.
In my form, people sway like evergreen trees
    in a dim forest.
In raincoats, they collect raindrops.
I am the form they struggle against.
They also fight the fire in my speech,
the pain from my gunfire,
the nightmare of my sleep, my dreams,
the words, like food, I force into their mouths.

None of It Was

it was a long
time before I saw
anything. Like

a seashore, even
the stockyards 5
blocks away. But

close, and not
a lie: was the
pool of blood—

animal blood. I saw
a long line of gulls
early, taste now
even their cry.

But none of it is
fumbled together,
reflecting some-

thing singular. Nor
was there in any
of it, a crisis.

Dismal Moment, Passing

    this is has to be here
because I am dis-
consolated.

        Even summer coming
4 years ago, now enlarges the green
accuracy of nature,
        which we won't see till Mexico, any-
way. I think of my mother when I think
of nature, her beliefs. Those lies in space
hanging there to arrange
human minds like suffixes to structures,
like societies. Or meaning like a sheet flapping
on a back porch, people might still
wash things, hang them up to dry. Like children
playing roots or shock on the side—
where we walk, upsidedown looking at jets go

        not easy like me here, in this opaque opening.
And promise to be All Right
tomorrow, yes yes

Vietnam

he was just back
from the war

said man they got
whites

over there now
fighting
us

and blacks over there
too

fighting us

and we can't tell
our whites
from the others

nor our blacks
from the others

& everybody
is just killing

& killing
like crazy

Michael Harper

We Assume: On the Death of Our Son, Reuben Masai Harper

We assume
that in 28 hours,
lived in a collapsible isolette,
you learned to accept pure oxygen
as the natural sky;
the scant shallow breaths
that filled those hours
cannot, did not make you fly—
but dreams were there
like crooked palmprints on
the twin-thick windows of the nursery—
in the glands of your mother.

We assume
the sterile hands
drank chemicals in and out
from lungs opaque with mucus,
pumped your stomach,
eeked the bicarbonate in
crooked, green-winged veins,
out in a plastic mask;

A woman who'd lost her first son
consoled us with an angel gone ahead
to pray for our family—
gone into that sky

seeking oxygen,
gone into autopsy,
a fine brown powdered sugar,
a disposable cremation:

We assume
you did not know we loved you.

David Henderson

Walk with De Mayor of Harlem

I

enter harlem
to walk from the howling cave
called the "A" train
from columbus circle
                (find america discovered)
all along a 66 block artillery blitz
                        to the quarter/
      nonstop
        existential TWA nightcoach
rome to auschwitz express
where multitudes vomit   pass out
witness death by many stabbings
upon pompeii/
            please close the doors please
before the madness of washington heights
      disembark   /silent moot   of black vectors
to sunder this quarter
                thru

black mass
black land

-of rhythm n
         blues & fish of jesus frying across the boardwalk
snake dancers walk mojo along wide boulevards

sight for those
              who live away
a new land!
no dream stuff
   in dem black neon clouds of de full moon
                to illume by sun-ra
streets just like you
              no thinking you crazy
vertigo
     under skyscrapers/

II

where harlem lies
        find no industrial green
                          giants
only
    bojangling children in the streets
only
    the sleeping car brotherhood of underground males
only
    the knights of the mystic sea
find only
       the black sapphires
       of the beulah baptist methodist church on the
                                mount
here
    clustered & cross-purposed

                     you can take it where you find it
                     or you can leave it like it is

walk with de mayor of harlem
find no   find no
                find not
many of the millions

of the downtown boston blackies
fancy of james bond
in psychedelic robert hall clothing
suitable drape for sawed-off
shotguns
under the trench coat

talk to me   talk to me
                        tell me like it is
the memory   of sky watch
sun dance   drum chant   body-ruba
taut are the signals thru the skin
thru bones
hard as the forgotten legions
of
the giant bushmen

O beaulah baptist in the streets/
to the paradise songs of bloodletting
the gospel singers   are   asayin/
the world is in a troubled time
when
        the knights of the mystic sea
clash
        with the sicilian asphalt paving company
a blood ruckus
                will ensue
that night
there will be monsoon rains over harlem
black panther bonnevilles prowling
from block to block
helicopters colliding with tenements
                                in orange surprise

Don L. Lee

Mixed Sketches

u feel that way sometimes
wondering:
as a nine year old sister
with burned out hair oddly
smiles at you and sweetly calls you
brother

u feel that way sometimes
wondering:
as a blackwoman & her 6 children
are burned out of their apartment with no place
to go & a nappy-headed nigger comes running thru
our neighborhood with a match in his hand cryin
revolution

u feel that way sometimes
wondering:
seeing sisters in two hundred dollar wigs & suits
fastmoving in black clubs in late surroundings   talking
about late thoughts in late language waiting for late men
that come in with, "i don't want to hear bout nothing
     black tonight."

u feel that way sometimes
wondering:
while eating on newspaper tablecloths
& sleeping on clean bed sheets that couldn't

stop bed bugs   as black children watch their
mothers leave the special buses returning from
special neighborhoods
to clean their "own" unspecial homes.

u feel that way sometimes
wondering:
wondering, how did we survive?

Assassination

     it was wild.
     the
     bullet hit high.
                   (the throat-neck)
     & from everywhere:
          the motel, from under bushes and cars,
          from around corners and across streets,
          out of the garbage cans and from rat holes
          in the earth
     they came running.
     with
     guns
     drawn
     they came running
toward the King—
              all of them
              fast and sure—
     as if
     the King
     was going to fire back.
     they came running
     fast and sure,
     in the
     wrong
     direction.

We Walk the Way of the New World

1.

we run the dangercourse.
the way of the stocking caps & murray's grease.
(if u is modern u used duke greaseless hair pomade)
jo jo was modern/   an international nigger
              born: jan. 1, 1863 in new york, mississippi.
his momma was mo militant than he was/is
jo jo bes no instant negro
his development took all of 106 years
& he was the first to be stamped "made in USA"
where he arrived bow-legged a curve ahead of the 20th
       century's new weapon: television.
which invented, "how to win and influence people"
& gave jo jo his how/ever look: however u want me.

we discovered that with the right brand of cigarettes
that one, with his best girl,
cd skip thru grassy fields in living color
& in slow-motion: Caution: niggers, cigarette smoking
              will kill u & yr/health.
& that the breakfast of champions is: blackeyed peas & rice.
& that God is dead & Jesus is black and last seen on 63rd
       street in a gold & black dashiki, sitting in a pink
       hog speaking swahili with a pig-latin accent.
& that integration and coalition are synonymous,
& that the only thing that really mattered was:
   who could get the highest on the least or how to expand
   & break one's mind.
in the coming world
new prizes are
to be given
we *ran* the dangercourse.

now, it's a silent walk/a careful eye
jo jo is there
to his mother he is unknown
(she accepted with a newlook: what wd u do if someone
    loved u?)
jo jo is back
& he will catch all the new jo jo's as they wander in & out
and with a fan-like whisper say: you ain't no
                        tourist
                        and Harlem ain't for
                        sight-seeing, brother.

2.

Start with the itch and there will be no scratch. Study
    yourself.
Watch yr/every movement as u skip thru-out the southside of
    chicago.
be hip to yr/actions.

our dreams are realities
traveling the nature-way.
we meet them
at the apex of their utmost
meanings/means;
we walk in cleanliness
down state st/or Fifth Ave.
& wicked apartment buildings shake
as their windows announce our presence
as we jump into the interior
& cut the day's evil away.

We walk in cleanliness
the newness of it all
becomes us
our women listen to us

and learn.
We teach our children thru
our actions.

We'll become owners of the   New World
the New World.
will run it as unowners
for
we will live in it too
& will want to be remembered
as   realpeople.

But He Was Cool

      or: he even stopped for green lights

super-cool
ultrablack
a tan/purple
had a beautiful shade.

he had a double-natural
that wd put the sisters to shame.
his dashikis were tailor made
& his beads were imported sea shells
     (from some blk/country i never heard of)
he was triple-hip.

his tikis were hand carved
out of ivory
& came express from the motherland.
he would greet u in swahili
& say good-by in yoruba.
wooooooooooooo-jim he bes so cool & ill tel li gent
        cool-cool is so cool he was un-cooled by
           other niggers' cool
        cool-cool ultracool was bop-cool/ice box
           cool so cool cold cool
        his wine didn't have to be cooled, him was
           air conditioned cool
        cool-cool/real cool made me cool—now
           ain't that cool
        cool-cool so cool him nick-named refrig-
           erator.

cool-cool so cool
he didn't know,

after detroit, newark, chicago &c.,
we had to hip
         cool-cool/super-cool/real cool
   that
to be black
is
to be
very-hot.

Nikki Giovanni

A Certain Peace

it was very pleasant
not having you around
this afternoon

not that i don't love you
and want you and need you
and love loving and wanting and needing you

but there was a certain peace
when you walked out the door
and i knew you would do something
you wanted to do
and i could run
a tub full of water
and not worry about answering the phone
for your call
and soak in bubbles
and not worry whether you would want something
special for dinner
and rub lotion all over me
for as long as i wanted
and not worry if you had a good idea
or wanted to use the bathroom
and there was a certain excitement
when after midnight you came home
and we had coffee
and i had a day of mine

that made me as happy
as yours did you

When I Nap

when i nap
usually after 1:30
because the sun comes
in my room then
hitting the northeast
corner

i lay at the foot
of my bed and smell
the sweat of your feet
in my covers
while i dream

The Women Gather
(for Joe Strickland)

the women gather
because it is not unusual
to seek comfort in our hours of stress
    a man must be buried

it is not unusual
that the old bury the young
    though it is an abomination

it is not strange
that the unwise and the ungentle
carry the banner of humaneness
    though it is a castration of the spirit

it no longer shatters the intellect
that those who make war
call themselves diplomats

we are no longer surprised
that the unfaithful pray loudest
every sunday in every church
and sometimes in rooms facing east
    though it is a sin and a shame

    so how do we judge a man

most of us love from our need to love not
because we find someone deserving

most of us forgive because we have trespassed not
because we are magnanimous

most of us comfort because we need comforting
our ancient rituals demand that we give
what we hope to receive

    and how do we judge a man

we learn to greet when meeting
to cry when parting
and to soften our words at times of stress

the women gather
with cloth and ointment
their busy hands bowing to laws that decree
willows shall stand swaying but unbroken
against even the determined wind of death

    we judge a man by his dreams
not alone his deeds
    we judge a man by his intent
not alone his shortcomings
    we judge a man because it is not unusual
to know him through those who love him

the women gather strangers
to each other because
they have loved a man

it is not unusual to sift
through ashes
and find an unburnt picture

Revolutionary Dreams

i used to dream militant
dreams of taking
over america to show
these white folks how it should be
done
i used to dream radical dreams
of blowing everyone away with my perceptive powers
of correct analysis
i even used to think i'd be the one
to stop the riot and negotiate the peace
then i awoke and dug
that if i dreamed natural
dreams of being a natural
woman doing what a woman
does when she's natural
i would have a revolution

Mother's Habits

i have all
my mother's habits
i awake in the middle of night
to smoke a cigarette
i have a terrible fear of flying
and i don't like being alone
in the dark
sleep is a sport we all
participate in
it's the scourge of youth
and a necessity of old age
though it only hastens the day
when dissolution is inevitable
i grow tired
like my mother doing without
even one small word
that says i care
and like my mother i shall fade
into my dreams
no longer caring
either

Alice Walker

Expect Nothing

Expect nothing. Live frugally
On surprise.
Become a stranger
To need of pity
Or, if compassion be freely
Given out
Take only enough.
Stop short of urge to plead
Then purge away the need.

Wish for nothing larger
Than your own small heart
Or greater than a star;
Tame wild disappointment
With caress unmoved and cold.
Make of it a parka
For your soul.

Discover the reason why
So tiny human midget
Exists at all
So scared unwise.
But expect nothing. Live frugally
On surprise.

Burial

I
They have fenced in the dirt road
that once led to Wards Chapel
A.M.E. church,
and cows graze
among the stones that
mark my family's graves.
The massive oak is gone
from out the churchyard,
but the giant space is left
unfilled;
despite the two-lane blacktop
that slides across
the old, unalterable
roots.

II
Today I bring my own child here;
to this place where my father's
grandmother rests undisturbed
beneath the Georgia sun,
above her the neatstepping hooves
of cattle.
Here the graves soon grow back into the land.
Have been known to sink. To drop open without
warning. To cover themselves with wild ivy,
blackberries. Bittersweet and sage.
No one knows why. No one asks.
When Burning Off Day comes, as it does
some years,
the graves are haphazardly cleared and snakes
hacked to death and burned sizzling
in the brush . . . The odor of smoke, oak

leaves, honeysuckle.
Forgetful of geographic resolutions as birds,
the farflung young fly South to bury
the old dead.

III
The old women move quietly up
and touch Sis Rachel's face.
"Tell Jesus I'm coming," they say.
"Tell Him I ain't goin' to *be*
long."

My grandfather turns his creaking head
away from the lavender box.
He does not cry. But looks afraid.
For years he called her "Woman";
shortened over the decades to
" 'Oman."
On the cut stone for " 'Oman's" grave
he did not notice
they had misspelled her name.
(The stone reads *Racher Walker*—not "Rachel"—
Loving Wife, Devoted Mother.)

IV
As a young woman, who had known her? Tripping
eagerly, "loving wife," to my grandfather's
bed. Not pretty, but serviceable. A hard
worker, with rough, moist hands. Her own two
babies dead before she came.
Came to seven children.
To aprons and sweat.
Came to quiltmaking.
Came to canning and vegetable gardens
big as fields.
Came to fields to plow.

Cotton to chop.
Potatoes to dig.
Came to multiple measles, chickenpox,
and croup.
Came to water from springs.
Came to leaning houses one story high.
Came to rivalries. Saturday night battles.
Came to straightened hair, Noxzema, and
feet washing at the Hardshell Baptist church.
Came to zinnias around the woodpile.
Came to grandchildren not of her blood
whom she taught to dip snuff without
sneezing.

Came to death blank, forgetful of it all.

When he called her "'Oman" she no longer
listened. Or heard, or knew, or felt.

V
It is not until I see my first-grade teacher
review her body that I cry.
Not for the dead, but for the gray in my
first-grade teacher's hair. For memories
of before I was born, when teacher and
grandmother loved each other; and later
above the ducks made of soap and the orange-
legged chicks Miss Reynolds drew over
my own small hand
on paper with wide blue lines.

VI
Not for the dead, but for memories. None of
them sad. But seen from the angle of her
death.

New Face

I have learned not to worry about love;
but to honor its coming
with all my heart.
To examine the dark mysteries
of the blood
with headless heed and
swirl,
to know the rush of feelings
swift and flowing
as water.
The source appears to be
some inexhaustible
spring
within our twin and triple
selves;
the new face I turn up
to you
no one else on earth
has ever
seen.

Medicine

    Grandma sleeps with
    my sick
        grand-
pa so she
can get him
during the night
medicine
to stop
  the pain

      In
    the morning
      clumsily
      I
    wake
      them

Her eyes
look at me
from under-
        neath
his withered
arm

  The
medicine
 is all
  in
her long
  un-
    braided
        hair.

Ntozake Shange

For Colored Girls Who Have Considered Suicide When the Rainbow's Enuf, Selections

    lady in blue
one thing i dont need
is any more apologies
i got sorry greetin me at my front door
you can keep yrs
i dont know what to do wit em
they dont open doors
or bring the sun back
they dont make me happy
or get a mornin paper
didnt nobody stop usin my tears to wash cars
cuz a sorry

i am simply tired
of collectin
        i didnt know
        i was so important toyou'
i'm gonna haveta throw some away
i cant get to the clothes in my closet
for alla the sorries
i'm gonna tack a sign to my door
leave a message by the phone
        'if you called
        to say yr sorry
        call somebody

                        else
                        i dont use em anymore'

i let sorry/didnt meanta/& how cd i know abt that
take a walk down a dark & musty street in brooklyn
i'm gonna do exactly what i want to
& i wont be sorry for none of it
letta sorry soothe yr soul/i'm gonna soothe mine

you were always inconsistent
doin somethin & then bein sorry
beatin my heart to death
talkin bout you sorry
well
i will not call
i'm not goin to be nice
i will raise my voice
& scream & holler
& break things & race the engine
& tell all yr secrets bout yrself to yr face
& i will list in detail everyone of my wonderful lovers
& their ways
i will play oliver lake
loud
& i wont be sorry for none of it

i loved you on purpose
i was open on purpose
i still crave vulnerability & close talk
& i'm not even sorry bout you bein sorry

   lady in red
i sat up one nite walkin a boardin house
screamin/cryin/the ghost of another woman
who waz missin what i waz missin
i wanted to jump up outta my bones

& be done wit myself
leave me alone
& go on in the wind
it waz too much
i fell into a numbness
til the only tree i cd see
took me up in her branches
held me in the breeze
made me dawn dew
that chill at daybreak
the sun wrapped me up swingin rose light everywhere
the sky laid over me like a million men
i waz cold/i waz burnin up/a child
& endlessly weavin garments for the moon
wit my tears

i found god in myself
& i loved her/i loved her fiercely

> *All of the ladies repeat to themselves softly the lines 'i found god in myself & i loved her.' It soon becomes a song of joy, started by the lady in blue. The ladies sing first to each other, then gradually to the audience. After the song peaks the ladies enter into a closed tight circle.*

HISPANIC AMERICAN POETRY

Rodolfo Gonzales

I Am Joaquín, Selections

I am Joaquín,
lost in a world of confusion,
caught up in the whirl of a
        gringo society,
confused by the rules,
scorned by attitudes,
suppressed by manipulation,
and destroyed by modern society.
My fathers
   have lost the economic battle
and won
   the struggle of cultural survival.
And now!
   I must choose
         between
   the paradox of
victory of the spirit,
despite physical hunger,
         or
   to exist in the grasp
of American social neurosis,
sterilization of the soul
   and a full stomach.
Yes,
I have come a long way to nowhere,
unwillingly dragged by that
   monstrous, technical,

                industrial giant called
                        Progress
and Anglo success. . . .
        I look at myself.
            I watch my brothers.
                I shed tears of sorrow.
                    I sow seeds of hate.
        I withdraw to the safety within the
circle of life—
                            MY OWN PEOPLE.
I am Cuauhtémoc,
proud and noble,
            leader of men,
king of an empire
civilized beyond the dreams
    of the gachupín Cortés,
who also is the blood,
    the image of myself.
I am the Maya prince.
I am Nezahualcóyotl,
great leader of the Chichimecas.
I am the sword and flame of Cortés
                        the despot.
                    And
I am the eagle and serpent of
            the Aztec civilization.
I owned the land as far as the eye
could see under the crown of Spain,
and I toiled on my earth
and gave my Indian sweat and blood
        for the Spanish master
who ruled with tyranny over man and
beast and all that he could trample.
                        But . . .
        THE GROUND WAS MINE.
I was both tyrant and slave.

                    * * * * *

Here I stand
                before the court of justice,
                            guilty
for all the glory of my Raza
                to be sentenced to despair.
Here I stand,
    poor in money,
    arrogant with pride,
                bold with machismo,
                rich in courage
                    and
                wealthy in spirit and faith.
My knees are caked with mud.
My hands calloused from the hoe.
I have made the Anglo rich,
                yet
    equality is but a word—
        the Treaty of Hidalgo has been broken
        and is but another treacherous promise.
My land is lost
                and stolen,
My culture has been raped.
                I lengthen
        the line at the welfare door
and fill the jails with crime.
        These then
are the rewards
            this society has
for sons of chiefs
            and kings
            and bloody revolutionists,
who
gave a foreign people
        all their skills and ingenuity
to pave the way with brains and blood

for
those hordes of gold-starved
                                strangers,
who
changed our language
and plagiarized our deeds
                    as feats of valor
                    of their own.
They frowned upon our way of life
    and took what they could use.
                Our art,
                our literature,
                our music, they ignored—
so they left the real things of value
and grabbed at their own destruction
                by their greed and avarice.
They overlooked that cleansing fountain of
                nature and brotherhood
    which is Joaquín.
            The art of our great señores,
                    Diego Rivera,
                    Siqueiros,
                    Orozco, is but
another act of revolution for
        the salvation of mankind.
    Mariachi music, the
        heart and soul
        of the people of the earth,
        the life of the child,
        and the happiness of love.
The corridos tell the tales
    of life and death,
            of tradition,
        legends old and new,
        of joy
            of passion and sorrow

of the people—who I am.
I am in the eyes of woman,
        sheltered beneath
her shawl of black,
        deep and sorrowful
        eyes
that bear the pain of sons long buried
        or dying,
        dead
on the battlefield or on the barbed wire
        of social strife.
Her rosary she prays and fingers
endlessly
    like the family
working down a row of beets
        to turn around
        and work
        and work.
        There is no end.
Her eyes a mirror of all the warmth
        and all the love for me,
and I am her
and she is me.
    We face life together in sorrow,
    anger, joy, faith and wishful
    thoughts.
I shed the tears of anguish
as I see my children disappear
behind the shroud of mediocrity,
never to look back to remember me.
I am Joaquín.
        I must fight
            and win this struggle
            for my sons, and they
            must know from me
            who I am.

Part of the blood that runs deep in me
could not be vanquished by the Moors.
I defeated them after five hundred years,
and I endured.
      Part of the blood that is mine
      has labored endlessly four hundred
      years under the heel of lustful
          Europeans.
          I am still here!
I have endured in the rugged mountains
  of our country.
I have survived the toils and slavery
  of the fields.
        I have existed
in the barrios of the city
in the suburbs of bigotry
in the mines of social snobbery
in the prisons of dejection
in the muck of exploitation
and
in the fierce heat of racial hatred.
And now the trumpet sounds,
the music of the people stirs the
        revolution.
Like a sleeping giant it slowly
rears its head
to the sound of
              tramping feet
            clamoring voices
          mariachi strains
        fiery tequila explosions
      the smell of chile verde and
    soft brown eyes of expectation for a
                  better life.
And in all the fertile farmlands,
            the barren plains,

the mountain villages,
smoke-smeared cities,
                    we start to MOVE.
   La Raza!
Méjicano!
   Español!
      Latino!
         Hispano!
            Chicano!
or whatever I call myself,
            I look the same
            I feel the same
            I cry
                    and
               sing the same.
I am the masses of my people and
I refuse to be absorbed.
               I am Joaquín.
The odds are great
but my spirit is strong,
                    my faith unbreakable,
                    my blood is pure.
I am Aztec prince and Christian Christ.
               I SHALL ENDURE!
               I WILL ENDURE!

Frank Lima

In Medias Res

In an instant
What falls from me is a matter of no concern
I push it away from me
I function when I eat
There is nothing more

My jaws slacken
I begin to move
The first knot of tension appears
My mouth grows inward

The directions are complete
Finally on one of my edges
There will be grateful silence

159 John Street

It will rain forever here
the buildings will be turned down
the artist will obscure the weather
the potters and the weavers
will rub the edges of the sand and
a wolf will come to the door
to explain the facts of my life

without illusion our jaws will lock
because it is a common attitude

when you limp
I think of your waterfall larger
than my birth

there are no essentials
about my life
the doctor was ugly
and the nurses were beautiful
a myth to the contrary is a lie.

Vacations

We have lost the planet to the block party.
It is dusk now and we strain our eyes,
something cool and being alive isn't enough
to warm your toes in an aeroplane.

I put my hands in the weather
and float the ashtray beside you,
magic, like the bubbles in beer
or mercury on a human face.

I want something wet in a glass.
I want three million years.

You float up like a sheep on the ocean,
hot tulips and bourbon,
I draw you like water from the sun
and swell the magnificent curtains.

Summer Wish

I take advantage of inventing women,
making them transparent and seducing them.
I complete the ritual by hanging up the phone.
Before the waves come to the door
and cover us completely let's take notes
of the bedroom.
I couldn't sleep
I dreamed she laughed at me all night:
"There are no people on the moon."
"Your wrinkles remind me of cars."
I greet you with breakfast
but you want lightning on the lake.

Hunter Mountain

The sky has the luxury of going anywhere.
The roads follow with the
gratitude of being abandoned
and watch the deer run through smoke.

This is the day of the animals' feeding on our waste,
the fatality of hands passing a soft spot,
the heavy breathing of small yellow animals.
This is my infancy:
three hours from New York,
a fall flexing of odors,
the desperate hunger in a car that sucks the air.

The expectancy of a garden full of wolves,
the face of a tiger in an ashtray.
I move and lie against someone
and plant light where I am correct.

This is the perfect place.
My children spin like bottles
because I am able to lie.
I smile in terror when they touch me.
The facts of my life remain facts.

I offer the guest no memories, no seasons.
The rusted cities of the sea gulls wash ashore
in some cocktail party like a large bird.

Have I stood over you with yellow eyes?
I was prowling your stark white floors at the bottom of the cage
with such brilliance that I have given up sleep.

I have run through my lungs

down down down into the water
where the fish bring light to the sun
waiting for the weakness of a dreamer.

Yellowstone

Before I tell you
of the stars
that keep you awake

like the thin jets
that hunt the buffalo

I want to stand in
front of you with
my gang of dreams

The ones that make
the mountains lose
their power.

Plena

During the day I play at drowning
looking for the smoke
of eyelashes and faded hair
the lilac shadows of blood
and the ruins of coffee
but at night
I dream of the last syllable
in my mother's heart
the last red word in her lungs.

Ricardo Sánchez

Toward

toward, toward, ever toward,
that infernal struggle to present
all the awesome realities of being;

lost, being, yet lost,
within the wintry madness
of marginal existence, looking
inwardly to find
that sentient sense
of my having been
more than an after-thought . . .

        soy como rayo de luna
        radiantemente enluzando
        las cavernas
        donde mi raza duerme

unaware that there can be more,
for it hurts to seek
and need
a jelling place
in which to express

        que tengo que vivir
        fuertemente/totalmente,
        como un pedazo de la historia . . .

I dreamt you last night
when far from your being i slept:
your lips caressed the sadness
gestated by separation,
o raza ardiente Chicana
you continue hauntingly existing
even here in this frozen nadir,
and a plethora of lies
lie furtively to my mind;

        no se puede decir
        que solo existo
        cuando nos vemos;
        no se puede admitir
        que solo vivo
        cuando nuestras realidades
        curten los momentos
        y cuando nos vemos cercas
        en los espejos de nuestras mentes . . .

yes, look at my many faces,
all the colors of my people
radiate out,
some scorched by the sun
and others
turbulently scowling,
yet i am
the silken facets of being . . .

        and when we seek out
        a reason for being,
        looking back atavistically
        at a past merging

all the realities
that we have been,

seeing our boredom becoming
the blood of pyramid and adobe hut,
and my language becomes another world,
and we converge
here from all the nation
to intone
all that we can be,
> es mas
> que momentos
> compartidos sobre cerverza y plática,

it is realization
seeping into mind and soul,
affirming that we can co-exist
but only if we care . . .

> so the struggle comes on,
> furious struggle demanding
> total capitulation,
> the loss of all i've been,
> relegating roots and causes
> to a dust-bin in the mind . . .

manic questions assail,
you, juan chicano or jaime boricua,
or robert chinee or richard injun,
any blackman or any other
name that projects out
your marginality,
just what in hell
can you presume to be?
can you be a universal latin
singing out
> the history of the oppressed?
or piano playing oracle
hosting

poet madness
amidst jack daniels drinking
with words of ease?

        or generalizing teacher
        striving to up-root/deracinate
        minds and souls
        from their sense of land,
and subtly announce
that only your way is right?

        mod hollywood producing chicano
        merged into asian fantasy
        mixt
        (irrevocably)
        with mandates
        from a concert master,
        stomped out into symphony
        that cacophonously proclaims
        that somehow we must merge
        and lose the differences
that make us
a diverse and human world . . .

        lost, my perdidos
        andamos versiculando
        bellezas
        dormidas
        como nuestras mentes . . .
and when we rap of barrio lives—
discarded
shards of non-technological perceptions—
we seek out those anchors
stabilizing
our anomic wandering selves,
and like all shipwrecked losers
we strive to standardize

                        feelings that know no measures,
                        for we exist as we exist,
but some get paid to standardize
and some do it out of fear
that without foundations laid by others
life will lose its meaning . . .
fear of dispossession
guides and ridicules our being,
living as i live,
knowing something is wrong
when i can dare to think
                                if only to myself
                        "thank god i don't exist
                        saying
                                god help me i'm ethnic,"
but truth it is,
for like all the people that i am,
i feel the need to be
much more than i can be,
lost and hurting that i am,
i view my loneliness
like others see their lives
                i am a shadow of my thoughts. . . .
lo que hoy me puede, carnales,
es tristesa del corazón—
el día que lo entierraron
yo estava hundido en prisión. . . .

I Remember

I remember a strong old man,
with wide shoulders, a full soul,
and words that illuminated my life

and such a man was
my father
strong and loving
like a lament sung/cried
or loving advice proclaimed
a man who was mature and masculine,
without fear of the world he lived;
my father
a real man
a proud chicano . . .
in those times . . .
when
present-day militants
were still conservatives.
he was already a protestor . . .

east el paso respected him,
barelas [a barrio in Albuquerque] knew him
in the birth of this century
    at that time he was number one,
    a chicano who never went back on his word,
was Pedro Lucero Sánchez
    his mother's maiden name was Gurulé,
and he was
    the father of el diablo barrio (in el paso);
he was one of the best junk yard dealers,
    nobody ever humiliated him,
his world admired him . . .
    this man was my father

what affects me today, my brothers,
is sadness of heart—
the day they buried him
I was submerged in prison. . . .

Pedro Pietri

Song Without Words

the windows of these thoughts
were blessed with insomnia,
I was still at the beach
a long time after we left
listening to the undercurrent
of your violet emotions,
I heard many flower gardens
whispering excellent music
to the sacred silence
on the breeze from the balcony
of the seven senses of darkness,
I have seen you before
in the essence of pleasant dreams
giving the sky flying lessons,
but it's just a room without lights
the melted calendar reminds me
"I know and I don't know"
I say to myself without saying
as the ocean forgets how to swim
when the wisdom of the waves
becomes aware of your tears
and the fact that the wind
became invisible when it learned
how to speak in tongues
to the rhythm of unending bridges
dancing with the shadow
of the integrity of your eyes

that get real blind to see
what their dreams are about,
so let it be unwritten
so let it be unsaid and unheard
we have nothing against nothing
that someday gets into something,
the highway was not high at all

Do Not Let

do not let
artificial lamps
make strange shadows
out of you
do not dream
if you want your dreams
to come true
you knew how to sing
before you was
issued a birth certificate
turn off the stereo
this country gave you
it is out of order
your breath
is your promiseland
if you want
to feel very rich
look at your hands
that is where
the definition of magic
is located at

Alma Villanueva

To Jesus Villanueva, with Love

my first vivid memory of you
mamacita,
we made tortillas together
yours, perfect and round
mine, irregular and fat
we laughed
and named them: ose, pajarito, gatito.
my last vivid memory of you
   (except for the very last
   sacred memory
   I won't share)
mamacita,
beautiful, thick, long, gray hair
the eyes gone sad
with flashes of fury
when they wouldn't let you
have your chilis, your onions, your peppers
   —what do these damned gringos know of MY stomach?—*
so when I came to comb
your beautiful, thick, long, gray hair
as we sat for hours
(it soothed you
my hand
on your hair)
I brought you your chilis, your onions, your peppers.

*translated from Spanish; she refused (and pretended not to be able) to speak English.

and they'd always catch you
because you'd forget
and leave it lying open.
they'd scold you like a child
and be embarrassed like a child
silent, repentant, angry
and secretly waiting for my visit, the new supplies
we laughed at our secret
we always laughed
        you and I

you never could understand
the rules
at clinics, welfare offices, schools
any of it.
I did.
you lie. you push. you get.
I learned to do all this by
the third clinic day of being persistently
sent to the back of the line by 5 in the afternoon
and being so close to done by 8 in the morning.
so my lungs grew larger
and my voice got louder
and a doctor consented
to see an old lady,
and the welfare would give you the money
and the landlady would remember to spray for cockroaches
and the store would charge the food till the check came
and the bank might cash the check if I got the nice man this time
and I'd order hot dogs and cokes for us
at the old 'Crystal Palace' on Market Street
and we'd sit on the steps
by the rear exit, laughing
        you and I

mamacita,
I remember you proudly at Christmas

time, church at midnight services:
you wear a plain black dress
your hair down, straight and silver
(you always wore it up
tied in a kerchief,
knotted to the side)
your face shining, your eyes clear,
your vision intact.
you play Death.
you are Death.
you quote long stanzas from a poem I've long
forgotten;
even fitful babies hush
such is the power of your voice,
your presence
fills us all.
the special, pregnant
silence.
eyes and hands lifted up
imploringly and passionately
the vision and power
offered to us,—
eyes and hands cast down
it flows through you
to us,
a gift.

your daughter, my mother
told me a story I'd never
heard before:
    you were leaving Mexico
    with your husband and two
    older children, pregnant
    with my mother.
    the U.S. customs officer
    undid everything you so

preciously packed, you
took a sack, blew it up
and when he asked about
the contents of the sack,
well, you popped it with
your hand and shouted
   MEXICAN AIR!*

aiiiiiiiiii mamacita, Jesus,
I won't forget my visions and reality.
to lie, to push, to get
just isn't
enough.

Untitled

you cannot leave
my aunt's house
without a
full stomach
   she would be
   offended;
she's small
and earth color, her
face records
her mother's people
   the hills and desert of Sonora.
her eyes hold
an eclipse
   of clarity/pain:
     once,
       when I was small
   I remember
     her and I eating
       a cluster of grapes
         in a matter of minutes
     each one so delicious
       we couldn't wait
        for the next, and
      when the last
        grape was gone
          we laughed because
            the grape:s skeleton
              looked so funny—
before she was born
her father recognized
her mother and converted (he was a minister)
and married her; his indian
blood mixed with that

of the spanish
conqueror. I saw a
picture of his congregation
in Mexico, his wife's brother
holding their first born
who died before five,
and the majority of his
followers indian/eyes stared
out at me and I
recognized them,
   my aunt, not yet born
among them.

I grew up hearing
my aunt's visions and dreams,
she had no one but
a child to tell them to —
she saw the bombing
of Japan and the
back of God
   and a neighbor's son opened
the front door and called her
the day he was reported missing
in action, and she
dreamt my house and knew
where the trees stood before
she ever came—and she's
always apologetic for staying
'too long' and she's always
sorry you're leaving 'too soon'—
   talking and telling in spanish
to english
in english for the skeleton
in spanish for the flesh
we sit for hours
   she being older for awhile

I being oldest in my turn
taking turns as we've
always done—
and she tells me
she tried going to
an anglo church, but their
faces were blank
and their
eyes
mute; they did not
recognize her—
and with the spontaneity of
a laugh held long
within her
　　she smiles
as she tell mes:
　　　—Mi gente son el color de la tierra.—*
and the clarity overshadows
the pain.

　　and she lapses and offers
me a cup of coffee and I
drink it or she
will be
offended.

*My people are the color of the earth.

I Was Always Fascinated

I was always fascinated
with lights then,
with my hands
with my fingers
with my fingertips, because

if I squinted my eyes at them
lights sprayed off
burst off
and a joy burst inside me
and it felt good on my
eyes to see it, so

I squinted my eyes at
everything in this manner
and everything had joy
on it, in it. it was
my secret. only

my grandma knew. I knew
she knew by the way
she looked at things
long and slow and peaceful
and her face would shine, lights
all over, coming out of
her tiniest wrinkles;
she became a young girl.
there were things that could not
shine lights. we
avoided these. these things
had no joy
gave no joy. these things
took joy. these things

could make you old. I didn't
know it then, but

these things were death.

Miguel Piñero

There Is Nothing New in New York

No hay nada nuevo en nueva york
There is nothing new in new york
I tell you in english
I tell you in spanish
the same situation of oppression
it's the only action in all the corners
of this nation
a revolver ghetto shooting
cold bullets against the police
luck is death which comes and has
the same stench of
poverty

There is nothing new in new york
brother don't stick your nose into welfare
believe me because the tar is ugly
and a curse that's a lot of fun
for the investigators

There is nothing new in new york
we solicit and need
a rain of solution
another work of revolution
a second movement.

There is nothing new in new york
bro work without bread

in this poetry factory
to contract and end the station of
this glorious nation is no game
brotherman believe it today and not tomorrow
that
there is nothing new in new york.

Alurista

What for?/Pa'Victor Hara

o

what for the rush
    and bloody pain?
what for the wars
    fought in your name?
what for our lord
    lord of our dawn?
    lady of our peace?
what for we die?
        listen my daughter hear me
        well, "what for the rain
        fall from the clouds?
        what for the flowers
        bloom in spring?
        what for our life on
        earth at all?"
            listen my son and hear me
            well, "what for the struggle
            in our hearts?
            what for on earth there is
            no peace?
            what for of death
            we are afraid?"

oo

what for my lord
allende died?
what for my lady
chile weeps?
what for our struggle
here on earth?
what for the empires
chain our hearts?
      "what for o'daughter, people
        seek?
      what for to own
        material wealth?
      what for the powder
        and the guns?
      what for play god
        by taking life?"
  "what for my son
we till the earth?
what for its fruits
    are sold, not shared?
    what for our homes
    are owned by few?
    what for we buy
    our burial ground?"

ooo

    what for, we know!
    allende lives
    we see the dawn
    shine through the lies
    what for the struggle
    in our lives

                    if not to make
                    all pueblos rise!
to you our lord
  we shall return
in ships of serpents
  we will come
                    to you our lady
                        we come back
                        flying with eagles
                        for our guides
            what for the ecstasy
            of our joy
            what for the warrior
            path we walk
            what for our lord
                lord of our dawn
                lady of our peace
            to unchain

        oooo

to free our minds
    to free our land
to free all pueblos
    to create
                        the nationchild of light
                            has come
                        and it resides within
                            our heart
                        to heal and lift
                            the nationhoop
                        with the power
                            of our love
we got to cross
    them blood red mountains
we got to cross

> them by ourselves
nobody else
> will cross them for us
we got to cross them
> by ourselves

In the Barrio

in the barrio
—on fiery afternoons
when the dusk prowls
    in the deserted street
well the mothers and fathers
    work
        —often late hours
after school
    we play marbles
in the playground
    abandoned and dark
without lights
    until night
we play marbles
    until we grow
to make our own party; a wild time
and walk the streets
with lights
paved—with buildings
as tall as the fire
    —the one that courses through my veins

When Raza?

when raza?
when . . .
    yesterday's gone
and
    mañana
mañana doesn't come
    for he who waits
no morrow
    only for he who is now
to whom when equals now
he will see a morrow
mañana la Raza
    la gente que espera
no verá mañana
our tomorrow es hoy

    ahorita
que VIVA LA RAZA
    mi gente
our people to freedom
    when?
now, ahorita define tu
    mañana hoy

Victor Hernandez Cruz

Today Is a Day of Great Joy

when they stop poems
in the mail   & clap
their hands & dance to
them
when women become pregnant
by the side of poems
the strongest sounds   making
the river go along

it is a great day

as poems fall down to
movie crowds   in restaurants
in bars

when poems start to
knock down walls   to
choke politicians
when poems scream &
begin to break the air

that is the time of
true poets   that is
the time of greatness

a true poet   aiming
poems   & watching things
fall to the ground

it is a great day.

Snag

1
i thought of you
early morning
my eyes still not open
your eyes leaning against the wall
& the beautymark behind your knee

(but i'm making this up; am i)

the way you threw your arms
into my coat
& yelled it's too big
but did not matter

anyway
it's early morning

2
who are they over there
singing in a corner
beer cans in hands
passing Luchow's
not looking in to see their boss
or to smell the food

early Sunday mornings
i do things like this
or i think of something better.

Aleida Rodríguez

*Exploraciones
Bronchitis: The Rosario Beach House

1.
al amanecer   el monstruo del mar dormía
and the sea would lick at the edge
with flat tongues of mercury   quiet and slow
después de leche con café
y pan con mantequilla   mi abuela and I
would go into the water   antes de los otros
she walked easily in the ocean   caminaba
conmigo en sus brazos   the sound of her large legs
parting the water   the legs that later I see
in the sun with sea salt drying white
on her skin   cruzada
con ríos rojos y azules
in her black bathing suit

ella en su gordura   floated in the water
como un globo o una ballena   I liked
her way without fear   no como mi mamá
who has always feared water in such abundance
the bath water, no   ni la de lavar las ropas
en el patio   but the ocean, yes
that was one thing out of her influence
but over the sand bars   caminaba
su madre   carrying me
to where seemed to be the end of the ocean
my arms around her neck

sometimes the water would reach my back
a veces más baja but always warm
and so clear   que mirando para abajo
I could see the strong feet of mi abuela
on the white sand   firmes
en agua como si en la tierra

2.
the middle part of the day
I spent con los niños de los vecinos
or others who came to visit   el día
siempre era pasado en chores
y chancletas de goma   running
after the melcocha vendor
who passed dressed in white for the heat
with those long, pointed candies
the color of azucar quemada
or following a straight line
along the water until we reached
la parte más remota de la playa
more sand than houses
las casas misteriosas
we imagined that brujas or locos
lived in them
out here   so far

3.
la regularidad de esos días
was broken once a week   when mi tío Guicho
would come to take me   a la ciudad
para mis inyecciones   in his '46 dust covered
chevrolet that was really black underneath
por el camino pasabamos fincas
fields cupping water   I didn't understand
mi tío Guicho would say: es bueno para el arroz
arroz

arroz
erre con erre cigarro
erre con erre barril
rápido corren los carros
por la línea del ferrocarril
I chanted quietly until we reached the clinic
where I extended the same arm each time

al regresar   muchas millas de la playa
I would stick my head out the window
I knew I was the one who could
smell it farthest away
yo decía: puedo oler el mar

there were three long folds of skin
on either side of his mouth
when mi tío Guicho laughed

4.
por la tarde
nosotros y los vecinos   would drift
out of our houses to fish
todos nos sentábamos a la orilla
on large barnacled posts nailed to the edge
with ladders reaching to the water
our padres or abuelos   smoking
their tabacos to one side of their mouths

la gradual caída del sol
made us swallow our words
as if we were the ones swallowing the sun
aveces uno u otro gritaba   feeling
the rod slip in his hand
los niños corríamos a ver
to see the media luna that had been caught
always the same   all of them with eyes that never closed

without speaking   nosotros, los niños
would draw our feet from the water
as long rectangles of light stretched
from the houses across the gravel road
and to our backs   we knew
that water could swallow you
into nightmares now   it was the place
out of where night rose and was absorbed
into the air   era la hora
cuando no se podía confiar en el mar
o en las cosas familiares del día

we made the world smaller
and brought it inside in our buckets
with the blue and silver fish
we fried in manteca
until the eyes turned white
like the nieve we had never seen

5.
the house trembled with my coughs
y los respiros de mis fantasmas de noche

Miguel Algarín

Sunday, August 11, 1974

    Sunday afternoon and it is one-thirty and all the churchgoing latinos have crossed themselves and are now going home to share in the peace of the day, pan y mantequilla, una taza de café and many sweet recollections of el rinconcito en Juncos, donde Carmencita, María y Malén jugaban y peleaban.
    Sunday afternoon and it is one-thirty and all the churchgoing latinos fuse each other with love and the women dress so clean and pure and the children walk so straight and pure and the fathers look so proud and pure and everything so right and pure and even as I wake up to my nephew's voice coming through the window, there is pleasure in awakening. My mother and father and Grafton and Johnny come in, there is light in
their eyes,
there is pleasure in living,
there is no shame in being
full of love,
there is no shame in being
nude while my mother's
eyes look in at me,
looking at my nude body,
body that she made mixing her blood
with my father's,
and there's no rushing for clothes
just sweet openness in being
loved by my family.

Sunday afternoon and it is
one-thirty and all the church-
going latinos have crossed themselves
and my body swings free.

Teresa Palomo Acosta

My Mother Pieced Quilts

they were just meant as covers
in winters
as weapons
against pounding january winds

but it was just that every morning I awoke to these
october ripened canvases
passed my hand across their cloth faces
and began to wonder how you pieced
all these together
these strips of gentle communion cotton and flannel nightgowns
wedding organdies
dime store velvets

how you shaped patterns square and oblong and round
positioned
balanced
then cemented them
with your thread
a steel needle
a thimble

how the thread darted in and out
galloping along the frayed edges, tucking them in
as you did us at night
oh how you stretched and turned and re-arranged
your michigan spring faded curtain pieces

my father's santa fe work shirt
the summer denims, the tweeds of fall

in the evening you sat at your canvas
—our cracked linoleum floor the drawing board
me lounging on your arm
and you staking out the plan:
whether to put the lilac purple of easter against the red plaid of
    winter-going-
into-spring
whether to mix a yellow with blue and white and paint the
corpus christi noon when my father held your hand
whether to shape a five-point star from the
somber black silk you wore to grandmother's funeral

you were the river current
carrying the roaring notes
forming them into pictures of a little boy reclining
a swallow flying
you were the caravan master at the reins
driving your threaded needle artillery across the mosaic cloth
    bridges
delivering yourself in separate testimonies

oh mother you plunged me sobbing and laughing
into our past
into the river crossing at five
into the spinach fields
into the plainview cotton rows
into tuberculosis wards
into braids and muslin dresses
sewn hard and taut to withstand the thrashings of twenty-five
    years

stretched out they lay
armed/ready/shouting/celebrating

knotted with love
the quilts sing on

Americo Casiano

When Was the Last Time You Saw Mami Smile?

when was the last time
you saw mami smile?

i mean really smile,
just for nothing smile,
peace of mind smile,
humble smile.
can you remember?
i know i can't.

i remember her smiling
because you ridiculed her
in front of your friends
and she smiled cause
it was the thing to do.
                 / you thought it was cute
                 but inside she felt hurt,
                 ashamed, stupid.

and can you remember,
the last time mami smiled?

an old friend greeted her one day,
told her how good of a woman she was,
for raising such a fine family
and she smiled.

the old man didn't know
she sacrificed her life
for it to happen.
sixteen years for it to happen.
sixteen years, sixteen long years
working in the garment district,
all to see it happen.

to see her daughters become putas y tecatas
on simpson street and southern boulevard,
putas on university levels to americanized dreams
and her sons strung out on the holy bible
and themselves
           / ooow i'm bad
           got my rainbow colored playboys
           got my long layered haircut. . . .
           maybe next week i'll turn it into an afro
           naw brother . . . have you seen esos niggers lately
           wearing esos braids
           look like farina and buckwheat of the little
           rascals.

and when was the last time you saw mami smile?

i mean really smile,
just for nothing smile,
peace of mind smile,
humble smile.

you say you saw her smile the other day
           even though pops beat her up
           with a bat . . .
           after that he went to see his other woman.

there were three little boys running upstairs
after three little girls

and mami smiled
            for she knew,
            what it would lead to. . . .
            it happened to her.

paca sits on the third avenue el
with her legs open
and mami just smiles,
painfully.

you say you love to see mami smile
but really smile . . .
like when her grandchildren call her . . .
            abuela, abuela, abuela
in the middle of the night
because el cuco is after them.

hey but look,
she's smiling now
and i'll never make her feel bad again.
i'll always bring you flowers
to keep you smiling
and i'll see you every day,
keep your place clean
and, and, an . . .

"sorry son but we have to close the coffin"

pity i never had a chance to tell her,
te adoro madre mía. . . .

Carlos Conde

That's How I Was

That's how I was
I took advantage of the
afternoons
and in my hands
to share with

brothers of memory
brothers that still sleep

since my father died
we left that sun
our morning and our
sacrifice

today I look in the mirror
with tears showing
and on the pupils of my eyes
and in my mind parade . . .

that taught me to be a man
and to know anger
and to confront everything
that I know he put there

like that child

to walk
some fruits
my little brothers
of yesterday, today, tomorrow

      —on Borinquen's soil

Life is a little changed
that was the symbol of our land

were left in the mountains
leaving my soul destroyed

. . . THOSE BEATINGS
from my old man

in my path

Sandra María Esteves

Blanket Weaver

weaver
weave us a song of many threads

weave us a red of fire and blood
that taste of sweet plum
fishing around the memories of the dead
following a scent wounded
our spines bleeding with pain

weave us a red of passion
that beats wings against a smoky cloud
and forces motion into our lungs

weave us a song
of yellow and gold and life itself
that lights a way through wildgrowth
burned in pain
aged with steady conviction
with bunions callouses and leathered hides

weave us into the great magnetic center
pulling your fingers into topaz canyons
a single lonely web glitters like a flash of thunder
your thumb feeling into my womb
placing sweatseeds of floral honey
into continuous universal suspension

weave us a song of red and yellow
and brown
that holds the sea and the sky in its skin
that holds the bird and mountain in its voice
that builds upon our graves a home
for injustice fear oppression abuse and disgrace
and upon these fortifications
of strength unity and direction

weave us a song to hold us
when the wind blows so cold to make our children wail
submerged in furious ice
a song pure and raw
that burns paper
and attacks the colorless venom stalking hidden
in the petal soft sweetness of the black night

weave us a rich round black that lives
in the eyes of our warrior child
and feeds our mouths with moon breezes
with rhythms interflowing
through all spaces of existence
a black that holds the movement of eternity

weave us a song for our bodies to sing

weave us a song of many threads
that will dance with the colors of our people
and cover us with the warmth of peace

NATIVE AMERICAN POETRY

Norman Russell

The Tree Sleeps in the Winter

the tree sleeps in the winter he
moves where the wind wishes him he
returns and he nods his head like
the child in the afternoon but he
cannot lie down

does the tree think thoughts
in the winter does he remember
the summer does he stand in
the snow waiting can the tree wait
as i wait?

do the trees speak down mountains do
they call shouts from the top snow
coming from the bottom saying the bear
sleeps do the trees listen
to each other?

does the tree sleeping feel the bird
scratching and scratching the squirrel
pushing his sleepy back the deer
rubbing his soft horn the sun
speaking saying come awake it is spring now?

There Is a Hungry Watching

the prairie tries to eat the forest
the forest tries to eat the prairie
i see some grasses in the edge of trees
like fingers of hands claws of paws
i see some small trees in the grasses
like toes of feet hands of arms

the prairie looks at the forest
the forest looks at the prairie
the prairie does not sleep
the forest does not sleep
there is a crouching waiting between them
there is a hungry watching between them

the people of the north wish to eat my people
the people of the south wish to eat my people
my people wish to eat the north and south people

the edge of the prairie the edge of the forest
are dying there is blood along the edge
the edges of all the peoples
there is blood there are dead bodies there

will there always be war between the prairie and the forest?

will there always be war among the peoples?

Jim Barnes

Last Look at La Plata, Missouri

The park, the heart, you see at town's center is soft
underfoot. All winter long the dying bluegrass
has fed on cicada bones, enough to fill a loft:

the drone of dying, constant cymbals and hard bass,
recedes to a waning echo in your ear. Each year
the town drops an inch or two in the mud, and has

little sense of its going, though a certain fear
of losing trade caused The Palace to buy a shade
and paint the yellow open sign and sell kids beer.

The town speaks of history, and goes slightly mad.
The silver jet, the town's only hero's joke it's said,
has lost a tire; the fuselage and wing tanks, glad

for past skies, are captive to flung rocks and love-red
names. Summer was too long and heavy for the white
bandstand warping above lost chords and maidenheads.

The town affirms its past. The druggist kills his light
above the store. A diesel moans toward Kansas City.
A lone dog barks. A child cries. All of winter night.

Lost in Sulphur Canyons

All the stones
unturned say
you are alone.

Not even a sun
cracks
the lead sky.

The deer
you thought
you tracked
has never known
the stones
you step on.

Stone by stone
you follow
the small water
down through
sulphur springs
rank as the fear
you try not
to taste.

For such descent
as this, you need
a guide, someone
to lean a word
or curse on.

Only the stones
know your breath
is wrong.

An absence
of wind grays
the pines
and your hair.

You stoop
to drink
your face.

The sweet, white
bite of water
leaves you stunned.

You smile to see
a face pale
against the sky,
a smile
you never knew
was there at all.

With all the hell
of sulphur and pitch
you know somehow
you couldn't be
happier, lost
as a stray dog
among the stones.

N. Scott Momaday

Carriers of the Dream Wheel

This is the Wheel of Dreams
Which is carried on their voices,
By means of which their voices turn
And center upon being.
It encircles the First World,
This powerful wheel.
They shape their songs upon the wheel
And spin the names of the earth and sky,
The aboriginal names.
They are old men, or men
Who are old in their voices,
And they carry the wheel among the camps,
Saying: Come, come,
Let us tell the old stories,
Let us sing the sacred songs.

Earth and I Gave You Turquoise

Earth and I gave you turquoise
    when you walked singing
We lived laughing in my house
    and told old stories
You grew ill when the owl cried
We will meet on Black Mountain

I will bring corn for planting
    and we will make fire
Children will come to your breast
    You will heal my heart
I speak your name many times
The wild cane remembers you

My young brother's house is filled
    I go there to sing
We have not spoken of you
    but our songs are sad
When Moon Woman goes to you
I will follow her white way

Tonight they dance near Chinle
    by seven elms
There you loom whispered beauty
    They will eat mutton
and drink coffee till morning
You and I will not be there

I saw a crow by Red Rock
    standing on one leg
It was the back of your hair
    The years are heavy
I will ride the swiftest horse
You will hear the drumming hooves

Duane Niatum

Chief Leschi of the Nisqually

He awoke this morning uneasily from a dream;
Thunderbird had crashed through
the jail wall like a club.
And from its circle, Nisqually women

led him back to their river, the dance of its song.
For a few changes in the wind
he burned in the forest like a red cedar,
his branches fanning blue flames
toward the white men taking the camas valley
for their pigs and cows.
Musing over wolf tracks, the offspring of snow,
the memory of his wives and children
keeps him mute. Flickering in the dawn embers,
his faith grows grizzly, tricks the soldiers
like a fawn, sleeping as the brush.
The soldiers make jokes about his fate,
frozen as a bat against their throat.
Still, death will take him

only to his father's burial mound,
past the rope's sinewy snap.
The bars lock in but his tired body; he will
eat little and speak less before he hangs.

Paula Gunn Allen

Grandmother

Out of her own body she pushed
silver thread, light, air
and carried it carefully on the dark, flying
where nothing moved.

Out of her body she extruded
shining wire, life, and wove the light
on the void.

From beyond time,
beyond oak trees and bright clear water flow,
she was given the work of weaving the strands
of her body, her pain, her vision
into creation, and the gift of having created,
to disappear.

After her,
the women and the men weave blankets into tales of life,
memories of light and ladders,
infinity-eyes, and rain.
After her I sit on my laddered rain-bearing rug
and mend the tear with string.

Kopis'taya
(a Gathering of Spirits)

Because we live in the browning season
the heavy air blocking our breath,
and in this time when living
is only survival, we doubt the voices
that come shadowed on the air,
that weave within our brains
certain thoughts, a motion that is soft,
imperceptible, a twilight rain,
   soft feather's fall, a small body
dropping into its nest, rustling, murmuring,
settling in for the night.

Because we live in the hardedged season,
where plastic brittle and gleaming shines
and in this space that is cornered and angled,
we do not notice wet, moist, the significant
drops falling in perfect spheres
that are the certain measures of our minds;
almost invisible, those tears,
soft as dew, fragile, that cling to leaves,
petals, roots, gentle and sure,
every morning.

We are the women of daylight; of clocks and steel
foundries, of drugstores and streetlights,
of superhighways that slice our days in two,
Wrapped around in glass and steel we ride
our lives; behind dark glasses we hide our eyes,
our thoughts, shaded, seem obscure, smoke
fills our minds, whisky husks our songs,
polyester cuts our bodies from our breath,
our feet from the welcoming stones of earth,

Our dreams are pale memories of themselves,
and nagging doubt is the false measure of our days.

Even so, the spirit voices are singing,
their thoughts are dancing in the dirty air.
Their feet touch the cement, the asphalt
delighting, still they weave dreams upon our
shadowed skulls, if we could listen.
If we could hear.
Let's go then. Let's find them. Let's
listen for the water, the careful gleaming drops
that glisten on the leaves, the flowers. Let's
ride the midnight, the early dawn. Feel the wind
striding through our hair. Let's dance
the dance of feathers, the dance of birds.

Robert J. Conley

The Rattlesnake Band

"don't wear that snake
for a hatband, boy,
you'll get struck by lightnin', sure."

        In the house of Thunder,
        Thunder's Son, the Lightning Boy,
        wound a rattlesnake round his neck
        to make a pretty necklace.

he walked with a swagger
& when he did, the rattles would sound.
ignore old superstitious men. be cool.

        The Lightning Boy
        flashed here and there
        around the ballfield—
        played circles all around
        his brothers—
        outnumbered two to one
        he won the game.

        There was once a time
        a hunter in the woods
        found himself surrounded
        by rattlesnakes
        the Chief—a very large one—spoke.
        "Your wife," it said, "just now

> has killed my brother.
> when you go home," it said,
> "make her go outside for water.
> And I will kill her."
> The hunter, though he loved his wife,
> did what the rattler said,
> and she was killed.

At the carwash
the boy with the rattlesnake band
was washing his car
when Lightning struck
the metal roof overhead

> One time in Cherokee country
> Lightning struck a house.
> a family of six
> lies cold in a single grave
> their names are listed there.
> "Killed by Lightning," it says.

On a shelf in the house
the hat with the rattlesnake band
is gathering dust.

We Wait

1. White Blight

Crookneck Whiteblight, anthropologist,
Bermuda shorts & tennis shoes,
spectacles on nose,
in radiant pomposity rares back
in his chair, feet on desk.
Of course, the songs themselves have small
value for the serious scholar, though I, my-
self, should probably acknowledge a certain
indebtedness to the savage for filling out
my biblio. But the real thrill is getting
the stuff they think in their childlike
simplicity is sacred. The successful anthro.
must be not only well-informed but *clever*.
And in the *cleverness*—ah, therein lies the
thrill. For instance, it's amazing what
the waving of a dollar bill can do; spirit-
uality goes up in smoke, so to speak, and
you've got yourself an article. I've had
not a few successes with the Amerinds.

2. The Earth

the earth is my mother
the grass is her hair
with your plows you are ripping her breast
I will not use a plow
nor will I cut the grass
nor herd and pen up my little brothers
the various animals
I cannot stop you
but I will not follow you.

3. (to be sung to the tune of
"A Mighty Fortress is Our God")

Is it not wonderful to think
What God has done for man?
He's sent the white to save the red,
To take him by the hand,
To take his hand and lift him up
From darkness and from Sin,
To teach him how to work and pray,
Speak English and drink gin,
To cut his hair a decent way,
Wear pants and shirts and shoes,
To eat his food with knife and fork
And gracefully to lose.

4. USA

the cities are overcrowded
with people who are going crazy
streams are polluted
a man cannot swim in them
nor drink from them
neither can he eat with safety
the fish that swim in them
the air is not fit to breathe
there is violence on campus
violence in the streets
the crime rate soars and
a senseless immoral war drags on
the government is corrupt
and does not even know it
and the English language is degenerating
on all fronts into Madison Avenue drivel
we have maybe 30 yrs. (they say)

5. the old prophecy

it came in various forms
from the Creek
& the Navajo
but the message is always clear
white men will come
(they did)
they will take the land
(they did)
they will nearly destroy the People
(they tried)
they will waste the land
(they have)
then they will go away
(we wait).

James Welch

Blue like Death

You see, the problem is
no more for the road. Moon fails
in snow between the moon
and you. Your eyes ignite
the way that butterfly
should move had you not killed it
in a dream of love.

The road forked back
and will fork again the day
you earn your lies,
the thrill of being what you are
when shacks begin to move
and coyotes kill the snakes
you keep safe at home in jars.

The girl let you out. She prized
your going the way some people
help a drunk to fall.
Easy does it, one two three
and let him lie. For he was blue
and dirt is where the bones
meet. You met his eyes

out there where the road dips
and children whipped the snake
you called Frank to death

with sticks. Now you understand:
the way is not your going
but an end. That road awaits
the moon that falls between
the snow and you, your stalking home.

Simon Ortiz

Survival This Way

Survival, I know how this way.
This way, I know.
It rains.
Mountains and canyons and plants
grow.
We travelled this way,
gauged our distance by stories
and loved our children.
We taught them
to love their births.
We told ourselves over and over
again, "We shall survive
this way."

The Serenity in Stones

I am holding this turquoise
in my hands.
My hands hold the sky
wrought in this little stone.
There is a cloud
at the furthest boundary.
The world is somewhere underneath.

I turn the stone, and there is more sky.
This is the serenity possible in stones,
the place of a feeling to which one belongs.
I am happy as I hold this sky
in my hands, in my eyes, and in myself.

What I Tell Him

I take my son outside
and show him a tree,
have him touch leaves,
this is a leaf, see,
it is green, it's got lines,
and it is shaped this way,
touch.
He touches the leaf
and branch trembles with his touch,
fat little hands roughly
and gently grasping what I show him.
Make him stand, bare feet,
on the ground, feel
that dirt, brown dirt and gravel,
solid clay, it won't grow seed
too well, have to have sand,
and leaves, sticks, manure,
and then it will grow things.
That's what I tell him.

To Insure Survival
for my daughter Rainy Dawn, born on July 5, 1973

You come forth
the color of a stone cliff
at dawn,
changing colors,
blue to red,
to all the colors of the earth.

Grandmother Spider speaks
laughter and growing
and weaving things
and threading them
together to make life
to wear;
all these, all these.

You come out, child,
naked as that cliff at sunrise,
shorn of anything
except spots of your mother's blood.
You just kept blinking your eyes
and trying to catch your breath.

In five more days,
they will come,
singing, dancing,
bringing gifts,
the stones with voices,
the plants with bells.
They will come.

Child, they will come.

Joseph Bruchac

Coming Back

When they woke me
tangled in their blue nets
the worm holes in my hands were gone

a bright painted boat
danced in the water
like a tethered colt

apparently
i had learned something
for i did not ask them why
or who i was
but stood
touched their hands and foreheads
and began to walk
up the golden sword's arc of sand

now
a thousand years
and two continents away
you wonder why my feet
move in dance to a distant drum

Gladys Cardiff

Long Person

Dark as wells, his eyes
Tell nothing. They look
Out from the print with small regard
For this occasion.
Dressed in neat black, he sits
On a folded newspaper
On a sawhorse in front of his blacksmith shop.
Wearing a black suit and white, round-brimmed hat,
My father stands on one side, his boy face
Round and serious. His brother stands
Like a reflection on the other side.
They each hold a light grasp on the edge
Of their daddy's shoulder, their fingernails
Gleaming like tiny moons on the black wool.
Each points his thumb up at the sky,
As if holding him too closely, with their whole hand,
Would spur those eyes into statement.
Coming out of a depth known as dream—
Or is it memory?
I can see inside the door where the dim shapes
Of bellows and tongs, rings and ropes hang on the wall,
The place for fire, the floating anvil,
Snakes of railroad steel, wheels in heaps,
Piled like turtles in the dark corners.
Long Person, you passed a stone's throw away from his door,
Your ripples are Cherokee prayers,
You carry the hopes of this nation within your banks,

You and he are alike, you are contained histories,
You are a generation of yet unbroken channels.

Combing

Bending, I bow my head
And lay my hands upon
Her hair, combing, and think
How women do this for
Each other. My daughter's hair
Curls against the comb,
Wet and fragrant—orange
Parings. Her face, downcast,
Is quiet for one so young.

I take her place. Beneath
My mother's hands I feel
The braids drawn up tight
As a piano wire and singing,
Vinegar-rinsed. Sitting
Before the oven I hear
The orange coils tick
The early hour before school.

She combed her grandmother
Mathilda's hair using
A comb made out of bone.
Mathilda rocked her oak wood
Chair, her face downcast,
Intent on tearing rags
In strips to braid a cotton
Rug from bits of orange
And brown. A simple act,

Preparing hair. Something
Women do for each other,
Plaiting the generations.

Liz Sohappy Bahe

Farewell

You sang round-dance songs.
I danced not to thundering drums
but to your voice singing.

You chiseled wood sculpture.
I watched not the tools or chips fly
but your strong hands carving.

You lived in a northern village.
I went there not to meet your people
but to walk where you had walked.

You followed calling drums.
I waited, willing the drums to stop.

Wendy Rose

Halfbreed Cry

My people cry ashes,
bleed fire from their eyes
like amber from polished wood
(the newly carved crucifix,
the twisted torso) as dying,
the tree searches its roots
for water
        and I feel it
        as a separation
        across which I stretch
        to almost touch them
turning
in the small space
of my life so distant oh
so very distant.

As natural as ants in a mound,
as geese in a cloud,
as seeds in a melon
they have each other
and here I come
like I could place
my own two hands
where by father laced up
the stones of his house,
        like I could sit
        at the tip of the mesa

and greet everyone home
by their most secret names.

I am over the canyon in one step,
down the highway, smelling the sea
and hearing distant thunder; I am leaving

my uselessness behind
for the people to use as they will
or to sell like a pot to a tourist
who would not know

the difference.

Story Keeper

The stories
would be braided in my hair
between the plastic comb
and blue wing tips
but as the rattles would spit,
the drums begin,
along would come someone
to stifle and stop
the sound
and the story keeper
I would have been
must melt
into the cave
of things discarded

and this is a wound
to be healed
in the spin of winter
or the spiral
of beginning.
This is the task—
to find the stories now
and to heave at the rocks,
dig at the moss
with my fingernails,
let moisture seep
along my skin
and fall within
soft and dark
to the blood

and I promise
to find them

even after so long
that underground
they have turned albino

to listen, to shine,
to wait with tongues shriveled
into blackberries;
and fearful of their names
they will crystallize,
burrow, become fossils
with the feathers on their backs
frozen hard like beetle shells.

But spring is floating
to the canyon,
needles burst yellow
from the sugar pine;
the stories
have built
a new house.
Oh they make us dance
the old animal dances
that go a winding way
back and back
to the red clouds
of our first
Hopi morning.

Where I saw them last
they are still—
antelope and bear
dancing in the dust,
prairie dog and lizard
whirling just whirling,
pinyon and willow
bending, twisting,

we women
rooting into earth,
our feet becoming water
and our hair pushing up
like tumbleweeds

and the spirits
should have noticed
how our thoughts wandered
those first days,
how we closed our eyes against them
and forgot all the signs;
the spirits were never
smart about this
but trusted us
to remember it right
and we were distracted,
we were
so new.

I feel the stories
rattle under my hand
like sun-dried greasy
gambling bones.

Leslie Marmon Silko

Toe'osh: A Laguna Coyote Story
for Simon Ortiz, July 1973

I

In the wintertime
at night
we tell coyote stories
                      and drink Spañada by the stove.
How coyote got his
ratty old fur coat
              bits of old fur
              the sparrows stuck on him
              with dabs of pitch.
That was after he lost his proud original one in a poker game.
Anyhow, things like that
are always happening to him,
that's what she said, anyway.

And it happened to him at Laguna
and Chinle
and at Lukachukai too, because coyote got too smart for his own
    good.

II

But the Navajos say he won a contest once.
It was to see who could sleep out in a
snow storm the longest

and coyote waited until chipmunk badger and skunk were all
curled up under the snow
and then he uncovered himself and slept all night
inside
and before morning he got up and went out again
and waited until the others got up before he came
in to take the prize.

III

Some white men came to Acoma and Laguna a hundred years ago
and they fought over Acoma land and Laguna women, and even
    now
some of their descendants are howling
in the hills southeast of Laguna.

IV

Charlie Coyote wanted to be governor
and he said that when he got elected
he would run the other men off
the reservation
and keep all the women for himself.

V

One year
the politicians got fancy
at Laguna.
They went door to door with hams and turkeys
and they gave them to anyone who promised
to vote for them.
On election day all the people
stayed home and ate turkey
and laughed.

VI

The Trans-Western pipeline vice president came
to discuss right-of-way.
The Lagunas let him wait all day long
because he is a busy and important man.
And late in the afternoon they told him
to come back again tomorrow.

VII

They were after the picnic food
that the special dancers left
down below the cliff.
And *Toe'osh* and his cousins hung themselves
down over the cliff
holding each other's tail in their mouth making a coyote chain
until someone in the middle farted
and the guy behind him opened his
mouth to say "What stinks?" and they
all went tumbling down, like that.

VIII

Howling and roaring
Toe'osh scattered white people
out of bars over Wisconsin.
He bumped into them at the door
until they said
           "Excuse me"
And the way Simon meant it
was for 300 or maybe 400 years.

Indian Song: Survival

I

We went north
        to escape winter
climbing pale cliffs
            we paused   to sleep at the river.

II

Cold water   river cold from the north
I sink my body in the shallow
            sink into sand and cold river water.

III

You sleep in the branches of
          pale river willows above me.
I smell you in the silver leaves, mountainlion man
              green willows aren't sweet enough to hide you.

IV

I have slept with the river and
            he is warmer than any man.
At sunrise
      I heard ice on the cattails.

V

Mountain lion, with dark yellow eyes
              you nibble moon flowers
          while we wait.

I don't ask   why do you come
               on this desperation journey north.

VI

I am hunted for my feathers
I hide in spider's web
               hanging   in a thin grey tree
                         above the river.
In the night   I hear music
               song of branches   dry leaves scraping the moon.

VII

Green spotted frogs sing to the river
               and   I know he is waiting.
Mountain lion shows me the way
               paths of mountain wind
               climbing higher
                         up
                              up to Cloudy Mountain.

VIII

It is only a matter of time, Indian
               you can't sleep with the river forever.
Smell winter and know.

IX

I swallow black mountain dirt
          while you catch hummingbirds
               trap them with wildflowers
               pollen and petals
                    fallen from the Milky Way

X

You lay beside me in the sunlight
        warmth around us and
        you ask me if I still smell winter.
Mountain forest wind travels east and I answer:
                taste me,
                    I am the wind
                touch me,
                    I am the lean grey deer
                running on the edge of the rainbow.

The Time We Climbed Snake Mountain

seeing good places
            for my hands
I grab the warm parts of the cliff
                    and I feel the mountain as I climb.

somewhere around here
     yellow spotted snake is sleeping
                  on his rock
                            in the sun.

so please,
     I tell them,
          watch out,
don't step on yellow spotted snake,
                he lives here.
                        The mountain is his.

Where Mountain Lion Lay Down with Deer
February 1973

I climb the black rock mountain
    stepping from day to day
                        silently.
I smell the wind for my ancestors
        pale blue leaves
        crushed wild mountain smell.
Returning
    up the gray stone cliff
    where I descended
                     a thousand years ago.
Returning to faded black stone
where mountain lion lay down with deer.
It is better to stay up here
                watching wind's reflection
                in tall yellow flowers.
The old ones who remember me are gone
            the old songs are all forgotten
and the story of my birth.
How I danced in snow-frost moonlight
            distant stars to the end of Earth,
How I swam away
                in freezing mountain water
          narrow mossy canyon tumbling down
                out of the mountain
              out of deep canyon stone
                      down
                  the memory
                  spilling out
                into the world.

Love Poem

Rain smell comes with the wind
    out of the southwest.
Smell of sand dunes
                tall grass glistening
in the rain.
Warm raindrops that fall easy
                     this woman
the summer is born.
Smell of her breathing
            new life
small grey toads   hopping on damp red sand.
This woman
      whispering to dark wide leaves
                        white moon flowers
    dripping little tracks in the sand.
Rain smell
      I am full of hunger
              deep and longing   to touch
wet tall grass, green and strong beneath.
This woman loved a man
            and she breathed to him her damp earth
song.
  I am haunted by this story   I remember it in cottonwood
                      leaves
    their fragrance in the shade.
  I remember it in the wide blue sky
      when the rain smell comes with the wind.

Ray Young Bear

The Way the Bird Sat

even for the wind there was no room.
the wind kept the cool to itself
and it seemed that his skin
also grew more selfish to feelings
for he was like a window
jealous of the light going through
denied his shadow the sun's warmth
when being alone brought him
the cool.

the way the bird sat
dividing the weather through songs
cleaning the snow and rain
from the underside of its wings
was evidence.
in its singing the bird counted
and acknowledged the changes
in the coolness of the wind.
he somehow held the bird responsible
as it flew about taking in puffs
of air.

often the image of blue hearts
in the form of deer crossed his mind
outdoing all magic and distortion
of the hummingbird who had previously
been the source of his dreams to follow.

now his thoughts took him out
into a cornfield where he felt himself
bundled up concerned about the deer
and their hearts.
the hummingbird who had been dodging

Joy Harjo

Someone Talking

Language is movement.
They watch the glittering moon
from the front porch in Oxford, Iowa.
Which reservation
in this river of star motion?
The man of words sits next to
Nonnie Daylight,
listening this time.
                Tequila, a little wine, and she
                remembers some Old Crow, yellow
                in a fifth on the drainboard. She
                thinks of Hobson in Oklahoma. And
                how he ducked behind the truck with
                her the summer powwow for a drink.
                Where is the word for a warm night
                and how it continues to here, a
                thousand miles from that time?
Milky Way,
And there are other words
in other languages. Always
in movement. He touches
her back where her hair
reaches to the middle. There
is that gesture and the
crickets voice beginning.
All in the same circle of space.
Maybe the man of words speaks

like the cricket.
Nonnie Daylight
hears him that way.
>	It is along the Turner Turnpike
>	between Tulsa and Oklahoma City, she
>	tells him,
>	where they have all those signs,
>	Kickapoo, Creek,
>	Sac and Fox.
>	Dating the beginning and end
>	of the United States recognition
>	of tribal histories.
>	And hell,
>	where is Hobson now
>	when she needs and tastes
>	the Old Crow.
>	Yellow fire all the way into
>	her belly.
>	The way they meant it.

They have maps
named after Africa and the blue oceans.
Sky circles the other way
but she doesn't feel dizzy.
Stars in the dark are clear
not blurred, and the earth's movement
is a whirring current in the grass.
The man of words outlines wet islands
with his lips
on Nonnie Daylight's neck.
>	She got stopped outside
>	of Anadarko once.
>	Red lights.
>	You must be Indian, said
>	the Oklahoma Highway Patrol.
>	Of course they knew the history
>	before switching on the lights.

                        And when they rolled open the truck
                        in the moist night,
                        Was only going home,
                        She said.
What voice
in the warm grass of her belly,
What planet?

3 AM

3 AM
in the albuquerque airport
trying to find a flight
to old oraibi, third mesa
TWA
     is the only desk open
bright lights outline new york,
                             chicago
and the attendant doesn't know
that third mesa
is a part of the center
of the world
and who are we
just two indians
at three in the morning
trying to find a way back

and then i remembered
that time simon
took a yellow cab
out to acoma from albuquerque
a twenty five dollar ride
to the center of himself

3 AM is not too late
to find the way back.

BIOGRAPHICAL NOTES

Miguel Algarin was born in Santurce, Puerto Rico. He is the author of *Mongo Affair* (1978) and *On Call* (1980), the translator of Pablo Neruda's *Cancion de Gesta* (*A Song of Protest*), the editor of *Nuyorican Poetry* with Miguel Pinero, and author of the play *Olu Clemente*. Algarin had directed the Nuyorican Playwrights'/Actors Workshop, and he presently teaches at Rutger's University.

Paula Gunn Allen was born in Cubero, New Mexico in 1939. She is of German, Lebanese and Laguna descent. She received her Ph.D. from the University of New Mexico, and has taught at the University of New Mexico. Her works include *The Blind Lion* and *Coyote's Daylight Trip*.

Alurista was born in Mexico City, Mexico in 1947, and arrived in the United States in 1961. He obtained his Ph.D. in Spanish and Latin American Literature at the University of California at San Diego. Alurista has recited his poetry throughout the United States, Mexico, Germany, Holland, and France. He has edited twenty-four books, currently is editor of three literary and academic journals, and has published six books of poetry including *return* (1982), *Spik in glyph* (1981), and *a'nque* (1979). Alurista presently is an assistant professor in Spanish at California Polytechnical University.

Liz Sohappy Bahe was born in Toppenish, Washington in 1947, a member of the Palouse tribe. She has attended the Institute of American Indian Arts.

Amiri Baraka (Leroi Jones) was born in Newark, New Jersey, in 1934. He was educated at Howard University. Baraka has founded the Black Arts Repertory Theatre in Harlem, and Spirit House, a community organization in Newark. He has taught at the New

School for Social Research, State University of New York at Stony Brook, and elsewhere. Among his poetry collections are *Preface to a Twenty Volume Suicide Note* (1961), *The Dead Lecturer* (1964), *Black Magic* (1969) and *Selected Poems* (1979). He also is author of numerous plays and prose works. Bakara's poetry is characterized by experimental stylization, original lyricism and impassioned racial pride. He has greatly influenced a generation of Black poets, a legacy comparable to Langston Hughes.

Jim Barnes was born in Poteau, Oklahoma, in 1931. He is of Choctaw and Welsh descent. Barnes holds a Ph.D. in Comparative Literature from the University of Arkansas and presently edits the *Chariton Review*, an international journal of poetry, fiction, and translation. He is currently Professor of Comparative Literature at Northeast Missouri State University. His most recent collections of poetry are *The American Book of the Dead* and *A Season of Loss*.

Ray Young Bear was born in Tama, Iowa in 1950, a member of the Mesquakie tribe. He is author of *Winter of the Salamander* (1980).

Mei-mei Berssenbrugge was born in Peking, China in 1947, but grew up in California and Massachusetts. She studied at Reed College and earned an MFA from Columbia University. Berssenbrugge has received two National Endowment for the Arts grants and the Before Columbus American Book Award. She has also served as a member of the literature panel of the New Mexico Arts Commission. Among her books of poetry are *Random Possession* (1979) and *Summits Move with the Tide* (1984).

Arna Bontemps was born in Alexandria, Louisiana, in 1902. He attended Pacific Union College and the University of Chicago. Bontemps served as librarian at Fisk University for over 20 years and as director of Afro-American studies at Yale University. His publications include *Personals* (1964), a poetry collection, plus a number of novels and several anthologies including *The Poetry of the Negro 1746–1970* (1970) with Langston Hughes.

Gwendolyn Brooks was born in Topeka, Kansas in 1917, but lived most of her life in Chicago, Illinois. She attended Wilson Junior College in Chicago. Brooks received the Pulitzer Prize for Poetry in 1950 for *Annie Allen*. Her other poetry collections include *A Street in Bronzeville* (1945), *The Bean Eaters* (1960) and *Selected Poems* (1963). Brooks also is author of several prose works and editor of two anthologies, *A Broadside Treasury* (1971) and *Jump Bad* (1971). She was named poet laureate for the state of Illinois in 1968, succeeding Carl Sandburg. Brooks has taught at numerous colleges and universities.

Sterling Brown was born in Washington, D.C. in 1901. He attended Williams College and Harvard University. Brown taught at Howard University for over fifty years, where he became professor emeritus. His publications include *Southern Road* (1932), a volume of poetry, and *The Negro in American Fiction* (1937) and *Negro Poetry and Drama* (1938), two works of literary criticism. Brown also edited a seminal anthology of Black American literature, *The Negro Caravan* (1941). His poetry is noted for use of the Black folk tradition.

Joseph Bruchac was born in Saratoga Springs, New York, in 1942. He is of Czech, English and Abnaki descent. Bruchac attended Cornell University and received his M.A. from Syracuse University. Bruchac has served as publisher and editor of the *Greenfield Review*, which principally publishes Third World and minority American poetry. Among his poetry collections is *Indian Mountain and Other Poems* (1971). Bruchac is editor of several important anthologies of minority American poetry, including *The Next World: Poems by 32 Third World Americans* (1978), *Breaking Silence: An Anthology of Contemporary Asian American Poets* (1983), and *Songs From this Earth on Turtle's Back: Contemporary American Indian Poetry* (1983).

Gladys Cardiff was born in Browning, Montana in 1942, but was raised in Seattle, Washington. She is of Welsh, Irish, and Cherokee descent. Cardiff attended the University of Washington, and has taught in the poetry program of the Washington State Arts Commission. She is author of *To Frighten a Storm* (1976).

Americo Casiano was born in Cabo Rojo, Puerto Rico, but grew up in the South Bronx. He has taught at Brooklyn College, where he was awarded the David P. Whiteside Award for poetry, and he has also won a New York State CAPS grant. His work has been published in the *Greenfield Review*, *Latin New York*, *Revista* and has been anthologized in *The Next World: Poems by Third World Americans* and *Nuyorican Poetry*.

Lucille Clifton was born in Depew, New York, in 1936. She attended Howard University and Fredonia State Teachers College. Clifton has taught at Coppin State College and several other colleges. She was named the poet laureate of Maryland in 1979. Her works include *Good Times* (1969), *Good News About the Earth* (1972), and numerous children's books.

Robert J. Conley was born in Cushing, Oklahoma in 1940, a member of the Cherokee tribe. Conley has served as a director for the Cherokee Nation of Oklahoma and as Director of Indian Studies at Morningside College. He has also taught at several other colleges and universities in both Indian Studies and English. Conley is author of *21 Poems*, *Adawosgi*, and *The Rattlesnake Band & other poems*. *Back to Malachi*, his first novel, is scheduled for November, 1986, publication by Doubleday with two more to follow, and his collection, *The Witch of Goingsnake & other stories*, will be published by the University of Oklahoma Press.

Victor Hernandez Cruz was born in Aguas Buenas, Puerto Rico in 1949, but moved to Spanish Harlem, New York City, in 1954. Growing up in New York he maintained contact with Spanish and English and uses both languages in his poetry. His work has appeared in such magazines as the *Evergreen Review*, *The Village Voice*, *Life*, and *The New York Times Magazine Section*. His books include *Snaps* (1969), *Mainland* (1973), *Tropicalization Reed* (1976), and *By Lingual Wholes*.

Countee Cullen was born in New York City in 1903. After attending New York University, he established his reputation at age twenty-two with the publication of *Color* (1925), a principal work of the Harlem Renaissance. Cullen also went on to receive his M.A. from Harvard University and published two more poetry collections, *Copper Sun* (1927) and *The Ballad of the Brown Girl* (1928). He also edited an important anthology during this same span of years, *Caroling Dusk* (1927). Cullen produced several more works prior to his death in 1946. He is known for his nonracial, romantic lyrics.

William E.B. Du Bois was born in Great Barrington, Massachusetts, in 1868. He attended Fisk University and received his Ph.D. from Harvard University. Du Bois was a leading scholar of Black American history, producing such works as *Suppression of the African Slave Trade (1896)* and *Black Reconstruction* (1935). His best-known work is *The Souls of Black Folk* (1903), which both prophesied and spurred Black movements for autonomy and civil rights. Du Bois founded the National Association for the Advancement of Colored People in 1909, and edited its *Crisis* magazine until 1934. He also is esteemed for initiating the Pan-Africanist Congresses, focusing on social and economic issues of African and American Blacks. Du Bois died in 1963 in self-exile in Ghana, Africa.

Paul Laurence Dunbar was born in Dayton, Ohio, in 1872. He was the son of former slaves from Kentucky, and his father had escaped by the Underground Railroad. He achieved national recognition with the publication of *Lyrics of a Lowly Life* (1896), the first poetry collection by a Black produced by a major publisher. The well-known critic William Dean Howells wrote an introduction for Dunbar's collection and was instrumental in advancing Dunbar's career. Dunbar went on to produce numerous poetry collections and novels prior to his death in 1906 of tuberculosis. He is best known for his dialect poetry.

Sandra Maria Esteves is a Puerto Rican, Dominican American poet, born and raised in the Bronx, who has been widely published in numerous anthologies and literary journals throughout the United States. She published *Yerba Buena*, her first collection of poetry, in 1980 and *Tropical Rains: A Bilingual Downpour* in 1984. Esteves was the recipient of fellowships from CAPS in 1980 and the New York Foundation for the Arts in 1985. She is currently the executive director of the African Caribbean Poetry Theater, which produces literary and theatrical events in New York City.

Nikki Giovanni was born in Knoxville, Tennessee in 1943, but was raised in Cincinnati, Ohio. She was educated at Fisk University and the University of Pennsylvania, and has taught at Rutgers University. Her works include *Black Feeling, Black Talk/Black Judgment* (1970), *My House* (1972), *The Women and the Men* (1975), and an anthology, *Night Comes Softly* (1970).

Rodolfo Gonzales is a former National AAU boxing champion, a world-rated boxer, a political organizer, and a political author. He is considered by many to be the father of the Chicano Movement, which was at its height during the sixties and seventies. He is the founder of the Crusade for Justice and Escuela Tlatelolco, a private school for Chicano youth. *I Am Joaquin* is considered the common cause and most inspirational epic of the Chicano Movement.

Jessica Hagedorn was born in Manila, Philipines in 1952, and arrived in the United States in 1962. She is author of *Dangerous Music* and *Pet Food & Tropical Apparitions*, which won an American Book Award in 1983. Her numerous plays and performance pieces have been produced extensively, most notably by Joseph Papp at the New York Public Theater. Hagedorn is currently program coordinator of literary events at St. Mark's Church in New York City.

Kimiko Hahn was born in Mt. Kisco, New York in 1955, of Japanese and German heritage. In 1981 she participated in the American Writers Congress, traveled to Nicaragua, and joined the Artists Call Against U.S. Intervention in Central America. Hahn received a fellowship from the National Endowment for the Arts in 1986. She is currently the poetry editor of *Bridge: Asian American Perspectives*.

Joy Harjo was born in Tulsa, Oklahoma in 1951, a member of the Creek Tribe. She attended the Institute of American Indian Arts, the University of New Mexico, and the University of Iowa. In addition to being a screenwriter and a tenor saxophonist for a jazz band, Harjo is an assistant professor of English at the University of Colorado. Her three books of poetry include *The Last Song*, *What Moon Drove Me To This?* and *She Had Some Horses*.

Frances E.W. Harper was born free in Baltimore, Maryland, in 1825. She was active in the abolitionist movement as well as other social reform movements. She is author of *Poems on Miscellaneous Subjects* (1854). She died in 1911.

Michael Harper was born in Brooklyn, New York, in 1938. He received an M.A. from both California State University and the University of Iowa. Harper has taught at many colleges and universities including Brown University. His many publications include *Dear John, Dear Coltrane* (1970) and *Images of Kin* (1977).

Robert Hayden was born in Detroit, Michigan, in 1913. He was educated at Wayne State University and the University of Michigan. Hayden taught at Fisk University for twenty-two years and also at the University of Michigan, and served two terms as poetry consultant to the Library of Congress. His many publications include *Heart-Shape in the Dust* (1940), *A Ballad of Remembrance* (1962), *Words in the Mourning Time* (1970), *The Night-Blooming Cereus* (1972), and *American Journal* (1982). He also edited an anthology, *Kaleidoscope* (1967). Hayden was elected to the American Academy of Poets in 1975. He died in 1980. Hayden's poetry is characterized by complex rhythms and human narrative portraits.

David Henderson was born in Harlem, New York City, in 1942. He attended the New School for Social Research, Hunter College and Bronx Community College. Henderson has served as editor of *Umbra* magazine and has taught at Columbia University and City College of New York. He is author of *De Mayor of Harlem* (1971).

Frank Horne was born in New York City in 1899. He was educated at City College of New York, Columbia University, the University of Southern California, and the Northern Illinois College of Opthamology. Among his careers have been optometry and service with the United States Housing Authority. He is author of *Letters Found Near a Suicide* (1925) and *Haverstraw* (1963). Horne died in 1974.

Langston Hughes was born in Joplin, Missouri, in 1902. He attended Columbia University and Lincoln University. Among his many publications are *Weary Blues* (1926), an important poetry collection of the Harlem Renaissance, *Shakespeare in Harlem* (1942), *Montage of a Dream Deferred* (1951), and *Selected Poems* (1959). Hughes also edited a number of important anthologies, including *The Poetry of the Negro 1746–1970* (1970) with Arna Bontemps, and *New Negro Poets: USA* (1964). He died in 1967 in Harlem, New York. Hughes achieved a reputation as a "poet of the people" comparable to that of Walt Whitman. His poetry is distinguished by the range of his subjects and styles, and by his commitment to Black dignity and American ideals.

Lawson Inada was born in Fresno, California, in 1938. He is of Japanese heritage. During World War Two, Inada lived with his family in the relocation camps set aside for Japanese American residents. Inada studied at Fresno State College, University of California at Berkeley, the University of Iowa and the University of Oregon. He has taught at Southern Oregon College. Inada is author of *Before the War* (1971), the first poetry collection published by an Asian American with a major publisher. He also is editor of *Aiiieeeee! An Anthology of Asian American Writers* (1975) with Shawn Wong.

Fenton Johnson was born in Chicago, Illinois, in 1888. He attended the University of Chicago. Several of Johnson's plays were performed in the Pekin Theatre in Chicago, Illinois. His poetry collections are *A Little Dreaming* (1913), *Visions of the Dusk* (1915), and *Songs of the Soil* (1916). He died in 1958. Johnson's poetry is characterized by his sympathy for the dispossessed and his use of free verse.

Georgia Douglass Johnson was born in Atlanta, Georgia, in 1886. She attended Atlanta University and received a music degree from Oberlin College. For most of her life Johnson was involved in government service in Washington, D.C., where she also hosted frequent Black writers' meetings. Her poetry collections include *The Heart of a Woman* (1918) and *An Autumn Love Cycle* (1928). She died in 1966.

James Weldon Johnson was born in Jacksonville, Florida, in 1871. He served as United States Consul in Nicaragua and Venezuela, and also as executive secretary of the National Association for the Advancement of Colored People from 1916 to 1931. Johnson compiled the first anthology of Black American poetry entitled *The Book of American Negro Poetry* (1922) at the start of the Harlem Renaissance. His best known work was a book of verse sermons entitled *God's Trombones* (1927). Johnson died in 1938.

June Jordan was born in Harlem, New York City in 1936, but was raised in Brooklyn, New York. She attended Barnard College and the University of Chicago. Jordan has served on the executive committees of P.E.N. American Center and the American Writers' Congress. She has taught at City College of New York, Connecticut College, Sarah Lawrence College, Yale University, and the State

University of New York at Stony Brook. Her many works include *Some Changes* (1971), *Things That I Do in the Dark: Selected Poems* (1977), an anthology, *Soulscript* (1970), and several novels and children's books.

Bob Kaufman was born in San Francisco, California, in 1935. He was an influential part of the Beat school of poetry flourishing in San Francisco in the 1960s. His poetry collections include *Solitudes Crowded with Loneliness* (1965) and *Golden Sardines* (1967). Kaufman's work is especially well-known in France.

Etheridge Knight was born in Corinth, Mississippi, in 1931. He was sentenced to Indiana State Prison in 1960, where he served eight years and where he wrote *Poems from Prison* (1968). Since his release, Knight has taught at the University of Pittsburgh, the University of Hartford, and Lincoln University. His other works include *Belly Songs and Other Poems* (1973) and *Born of a Woman* (1980).

Alex Kuo was born in Boston, Massachusetts, in 1939. He attended Knox College and the University of Iowa's Writers Workshop. Kuo has been the recipient of the Davenport Drama Award, the Greig Post Poetry Award, and grants from the National Endowment for the Arts. He has published poetry and fiction in more than one hundred journals. His books of poetry include *The Window Tree* (1971), *New Letters from Hiroshima and Other Poems* (1984), and *Changing the River* (1986).

Don Lee was born in Little Rock, Arkansas, in 1942. He attended Chicago City College and Roosevelt University. Lee has served as editor of the Third World Press in Chicago, Illinois, and has taught at Howard University. Lee established his reputation as a Black consciousness poet with *Think Black* (1967). His other works include *Black Pride* (1968), *Don't Cry, Scream* (1969), *We Walk the Way of the New World* (1970), and literary criticism, *Dynamite Voices* (1972).

Frank Lima was born in New York City in 1939. He is of Mexican heritage. Lima attended Columbia University, and has directed a drug rehabilitation program in New York City. His poetry collections include *Inventory* (1964), *Underground with an Oriole* (1972) and *Angel* (1976). Lima's poetic style is marked by surprising connections of thought and imagery in an urban environment.

Audre Lorde was born in Harlem, New York City, in 1934. She attended Hunter College and Columbia University. Lorde has taught at Hunter College, John Jay College of Criminal Justice, and City College of New York. Her poetry collections include *Cables to Rage* (1970), *Coal* (1976), *The Black Unicorn* (1978), and *Chosen Poems: Old and New* (1982).

Naomi Long Madgett was born in Norfolk, Virginia, in 1923. Her poems have been included in numerous journals and anthologies in the United States and abroad; some have been translated and several set to music and publicly performed. Madgett is currently professor emeritus of English at Eastern Michigan University. Her six volumes of poetry include: *Songs to a Phantom Nightingale* (1941), *One and the Many* (1956), *Star by Star* (1965, 1970), *Pink Ladies in the Afternoon* (1972), *Exit and Entrances* (1978), and *Phantom Nightingale; Juvenilia* (1981).

Clarence Major was born in Atlanta, Georgia in 1936, but was raised in Chicago, Illinois. He attended the New School for Social Research, and has taught at Sarah Lawrence College and the University of Colorado. Major also has directed the Harlem Writers Workshop and has served as editor of the *Journal of Black Poetry*. Among his works are *Swallow the Lake* (1970), *Symptoms & Madness* (1971), *The Syncopated Cakewalk* (1974), an anthology, *The New Black Poetry* (1969), and several novels.

Laureen Mar was born in Seattle, Washington, in 1953. She attended the University of Washington and Columbia University's School of the Arts. Mar writes poetry and fiction and occasionally

354 *Biographical Notes*

does guest-editing and consulting for magazines. She has won the Academy of American Poets Award, the Marie K. Dearborn Award, and the Pacific Northwest Writers Prize. She currently works in public relations for the Seattle Art Museum.

Claude McKay was born in Sunny Ville, Jamaica, British West Indies in 1891. While in Jamaica, McKay worked as a constable and produced two poetry collections, *Songs of Jamaica* and *Constab Ballads* (1912). McKay came to America and attended Tuskegee Institute and Kansas State College. He moved to Harlem, New York in 1914, and soon thereafter produced two more poetry collections, *Spring in New Hampshire* (1920) and *Harlem Shadows* (1922). McKay also traveled to the Soviet Union and France, and later became a public school teacher in Chicago, Illinois. He died in 1948. McKay's poetry is known for its bitter realism packaged in controlled sonnets.

Janice Mirikitani is a third generation Japanese American. She has worked as an editor for various magazines and anthologies, including *Ayumi: A Japanese American Anthology*, which is a bilingual collection. Mirikitani is author of *Awake in the River* and has been published in many anthologies and magazines as well. She is presently the program director at Glide Church/Urban Center where she encourages community participation in the arts.

N. Scott Momaday was born in Lawton, Oklahoma in 1934, a member of the Choctaw tribe. He attended the University of New Mexico and received his Ph.D. from Stanford University. He has taught at the University of California at Berkeley and Stanford University. Momaday's first novel *House Made of Dawn* won the Pulitzer Prize for Fiction in 1970. He is also author of *The Gourd Dancer* (1976), a poetry collection, *The Way to Rainy Mountain* (1969), prose, and *The Names*, an autobiography (1977). Momaday's poetry displays a strong presence of Indian folk tradition.

Alice Dunbar-Nelson was born in New Orleans, Louisiana, in 1875. She was educated at Straight College in New Orleans and married the poet Paul Dunbar Nelson in 1898. She and her husband promoted Black literature and arranged stage presentations of many works. Her prose and poetry was published in many periodicals of her day. Nelson died in 1935.

Duane Niatum was born in Seattle, Washington, in 1938. He is of mixed-blood and a member of the Klallam Nation of Washington State. In 1983 he was invited to participate in Rotterdam's International Poetry Festival. His poems, stories, and essays have been translated into more than nine languages, including Italian, Dutch and Russian. In 1975 he edited the anthology *Carriers of the Dream Wheel*. It has become one of the most widely read books on contemporary Native American Poetry. His latest collection, *Song for the Harvester of Dreams* (1981), won the American Book Award from The Before Columbus Foundation.

Simon Ortiz was born in Pueblo of Acoma, Albuquerque, New Mexico in 1941. He attended the University of New Mexico and the University of Iowa. Ortiz has taught at Navajo Community College, the University of New Mexico, and the Institute of American Indian Arts. Among his publications are *Going for the Rain* (1976), *A Good Journey* (1977), and *From Sand Creek* which won the Pushcart Prize for small presses in 1982.

Pedro Pietri was born in Ponce, Puerto Rico, in 1944. He is a poet and a playwright. His four books of poetry are *Puerto Rican Obituary*, *Uptown Train*, *Out of Order*, and *Traffic Violations*. Two of his plays have been directed by Jose Ferrer and another was premiered by Miriam Colon's Traveling Theater. Pietri has conducted workshops for C.E.T.A., SUNY at Buffalo, the New York State Council on the Arts, and El Museo del Barrio.

Miguel Piñero was born in Gurabo, Puerto Rico in 1946, but was raised in the Lower East Side of New York City. Piñero is author of

Short Eyes, a play produced by Joseph Papp at Lincoln Center in New York City and which won a New York Drama Critics Circle Award. He also is author of *La Bodega Sold Dreams* (1980), a poetry collection, and editor of *Nuyorican Poetry* (1975) with Miguel Algarin.

Dudley Randall was born in Washington, D.C. in 1914. He attended Wayne State University and the University of Michigan. Randall served in World War Two. He founded the Broadside Press in Detroit, Michigan, a major outlet for Black American writing. Randall also taught at the University of Michigan and pursued a career as a librarian. His works include *Poem Counterpoem* (1966) with Margaret Danner, *Cities Burning* (1968), and several anthologies including *For Malcolm* (1967) and *The Black Poets* (1971).

Aleida Rodríguez was born in Havana, Cuba in 1953, but immigrated to the United States in 1962. Her poems and short stories have appeared in *Who's Who in Poetry in American Colleges and Universities*, *Momentum Magazine*, *Chrysalis 9*, *L.A. Weekly*, and *Beyond Baroque 9*.

Wendy Rose was born in Oakland, California in 1948, a member of the Hopi and Miwok tribes. She attended Contra Costa College and the University of California at Berkeley. She also has taught at the University of California at Berkeley. Among her poetry collections are *Hopi Roadrunner Dancing* (1973), *Academic Squaw* (1977), *Lost Copper* (1980), and *The Half Breed Chronicles and Other Poems* (1985).

Norman Russell was born in Big Stone Gap, Virginia in 1921, a member of the Cherokee tribe. Russell received his Ph.D. in botany from the University of Minnesota, and has taught botany courses at numerous colleges and universities. He is author of numerous books both of botany and of poetry.

Ricardo Sánchez was born in El Paso, Texas in 1941, of Mexican heritage. He received a Ph.D. from Union Graduate School and has lectured in every state except Hawaii. Sánchez writes a weekly column on the arts for the *San Antonio Express News*. He also founded and directs the Poets of Tejas reading series in San Antonio. His recent works include *Selected Poems* (1986), *Perdido: A Barrio Story* (1986) and *Amsterdam Cantos y Poemas Pistos* (1983).

Sonia Sanchez was born in Birmingham, Alabama in 1935, but was raised in Harlem, New York City. She was a recipient of a National Endowment for the Arts grant for 1978–79, the Lucretia Mott Award for 1984 and was the 1985 American Book Award winner for her collection, *Homegirls and Handgrenades*. Sanchez has lectured at over five hundred universities and has traveled extensively, reading her poems in Cuba, England, the West Indies, Norway, The People's Republic of China, and Australia. She is the author of twelve books, a contributing editor to *Black Scholar, Journal of African Studies*, and has edited two anthologies.

Ntozake Shange was born in 1948. She attended Barnard College and received her M.A. from the University of Southern California. Shange is best known as author of the choreopoem *For Colored Girls Who Have Considered Suicide* (1977) which was produced on Broadway. A number of her plays have been produced by Joseph Papp's Public Theatre in New York City. Her other publications include *Sassafras* (1976), a novel, and *Nappy Edges* (1978) and *A Daughter's Geography* (1983), two collections of poetry.

Leslie Silko was born in Albuquerque, New Mexico, in 1948. She is of Mexican and Laguna descent. Silko attended the University of New Mexico, and has taught at the University of New Mexico and University of Arizona. She has been a recipient of a MacArthur Foundation award. Silko is author of *Laguna Woman* (1974), *Ceremony* (1977), and *Storyteller* (1981).

Melvin Tolson was born in Moberly, Missouri, in 1898. He attended Fisk University and Lincoln University and received his M.A. from

Columbia University. Tolson taught for over twenty years at Wiley College in Texas, and served four terms as mayor of Langston, Oklahoma. His works include *Rendezvous with America* (1944), *Libretto for the Republic of Liberia* (1953) which was commissioned for the centennial of the African nation and which earned Tolson the title of Poet Laureate of Liberia, and *Harlem Gallery* (1965). Tolson died in 1966. His poetry is highly learned and allusive.

Jean Toomer was born in Washington, D.C., in 1893. He was educated at the University of Wisconsin and City College of New York. Toomer established his reputation with the publication of *Cane* (1923), which skillfully intermingled both poetry and prose, and became known as a seminal work of the Harlem Renaissance. Toomer died in 1967 in the self-imposed obscurity of a Quaker community in Philadelphia, Pennsylvania.

Alma Villanueva was born in Lompoc, California in 1945, and is of Mexican heritage. She has won many awards for her verse, which has been anthologized widely. Villanueva's poetry is confessional and strongly feminist. She is the author of *Bloodroot* (1977), *Mother, May I?* (1978), and *Life Span* (1984).

Derek Walcott was born in Chastries, St. Lucia, West Indies, in 1930. He was educated at St. Mary's College and the University of West Indies. Walcott has served as director of the Trinidad Theatre Workshop. He is author of *The Star-Apple Kingdom* (1980) and *The Fortunate Traveller* (1981).

Alice Walker was born in Eatonton, Georgia, in 1944. She attended Spelman College and Sarah Lawrence College. Walker has been active in welfare rights and voter registration in Georgia and New York. She has served as an editor of *Ms.* magazine, and has traveled to Africa and the Soviet Union. In 1983 her novel *The Color Purple* won the Pulitzer Prize for Fiction and the American Book Award. Her poetry collections include *Once* (1968) and *Revolutionary Petunias and Other Poems* (1972).

James Welch was born in Browning, Montana in 1940, a member of the Blackfeet and Gros Ventre tribes. He attended the University of Minnesota, Northern Montana College, and the University of Montana. He has served on the Literary Panel of the National Endowment for the Arts. Welch is author of *Riding the Earthboy 40* (1971) and several novels.

Phillis Wheatley was born in Africa in 1753. She was enslaved at age eight to Mr. Wheatley of Boston, Massachusetts. At age twenty she published *Poems on Various Subjects, Religious and Moral* (1773), the first publication by a Black American. The collection achieved great success in England and the United States. The poetry is primarily nonracial in subject matter and emulates the neoclassical style of Alexander Pope. Wheatley died in 1784.

Shawn Wong was born in Oakland, California, in 1949. He attended San Francisco State College and the University of California at Berkeley. Wong has served as a director of the Combined Asian American Resources Project at San Francisco State University. He is editor of *Aiiieeeee! An Anthology of Asian American Writers* (1975) with Lawson Inada. Wong is author of several novels, including *Homebase* (1979).

INDEX

Poet names are in bold; poem titles are in italics; poem first lines are in quotations.

About the Reunion. June Jordan. 197.
Acosta, Teresa Palomo. 285.
African China. Melvin B. Tolson. 101.
"al amanecer el monstruo del mar dormía," 279.
Algarín, Miguel. 283.
Allen, Paula Gunn. 304.
"All the stones," 299.
"All the things. The objects," 176.
All the World Moved. June Jordan. 194.
"Although I'm oldest I can't," 35.
Alurista. 270.
"And God called Moses from the burning bush," 68.
"And last night a man came in," 12.
"And several strengths, from drowsiness campaigned," 159.
"And so for nights," 139.
"——And when you have forgotten the bright bedclothes," 156.
"the aspens yesterday," 6.
Assassination. Don L. Lee. 212.
"As the gook woman howls," 138.
August 6. Janice Mirikitani. 39.
Bahe, Liz Sohappy. 322.
"Bananas ripe and green, and ginger root," 86.
"Bare," 2.
Barnes, Jim. 298.
The Bath: August 6, 1945. Kimiko Hahn. 36.
"Bathing the summer night," 36.
The Bean Eaters. Gwendolyn Brooks. 158.
Bear, Ray Young. 337.
"Because there was a man somewhere in a candystripe silk shirt," 136.
"Because we live in the browning season," 305.
"Before I tell you," 247.
"Bending, I bow my head," 321.
Berssenbrugge, Mei-mei. 10.
A Black Man Talks of Reaping. Arna Bontemps. 126.
"Black reapers with the sound of steel on stones," 88.
Black Rocks. Laureen Mar. 33.

Black Woman. Naomi Long Madgett. 166.
Blanket Weaver. Sandra María Esteves. 292.
Blue like Death. James Welch. 312.
Bontemps, Arna. 122.
Brooks, Gwendolyn. 156.
Brown River, Smile. Jean Toomer. 91.
Brown, Sterling. 117.
Bruchac, Joseph. 318.
Burial. Alice Walker. 225.
But He Was Cool. Don L. Lee. 216.
Cardiff, Gladys. 319.
Carriers of the Dream Wheel. N. Scott Momaday. 301.
Casiano, Americo. 288.
A Certain Peace. Nikki Giovanni. 218.
Chief Leschi of the Nisqually. Duane Niatum. 303.
Clifton, Lucille. 193.
Close Your Eyes!. Arna Bontemps. 122.
Coal. Audre Lorde. 180.
Cold Term. Leroi Jones. 176.
Combing. Gladys Cardiff. 321.
Coming Back. Joseph Bruchac. 318.
Conde, Carlos. 291.
Conley, Robert J. 307.
"A connoisseur," 101.
"Crookneck whiteblight, anthropologist," 309.
Cruz, Victor Hernandez. 276.
Cullen, Countee. 134.
"Dark as wells, his eyes," 319.
Dark Symphony. Melvin B. Tolson. 96.
Daughter. Kimiko Hahn. 35.
The Debt. Paul Laurence Dunbar. 76.
Desert Flowers. Janice Mirikitani. 44.
Did You Not See. Alex Kuo. 6.
Dismal Moment, Passing. Clarence Major. 203.
Do Not Let. Pedro Pietri. 258.
"don't wear that snake," 307.
Dream Deferred. Langston Hughes. 132.
"Drifting night in the Georgia pines," 135.
Du Bois, W.E.B. 65.

361

"Dull unwashed windows of eyes," 178.
Dunbar, Paul Laurence. 75.
"During the day I play at drowning," 248.
Earth and I Gave You Turquoise. N. Scott Momaday. 302.
"enter harlem," 207.
Ere Sleep Comes Down To Soothe the Weary Eyes. Paul Laurence Dunbar. 78.
Esteves, Sandra María. 292.
"even for the wind there was no room," 337.
Expect Nothing. Alice Walker. 224.
**Exploraciones Bronchitis: The Rosario Beach House.* Aleida Rodríguez. 279.
Farewell. Liz Sohappy Bahe. 322.
"First, feel, then feel, then," 179.
Fish and Swimmers and Lonely Birds Sweep Past Us. Mei-mei Berssenbrugge. 11.
"Flowers," 44.
For Christopher. June Jordan. 195.
For Colored Girls Who Have Considered Suicide When the Rainbow's Enuf, Selections. Ntozake Shange. 230.
"Formalized," 29.
Form. Clarence Major. 201.
Frederick Douglass. Robert Hayden. 137.
Freedom. Langston Hughes. 133.
Georgia Dusk. Jean Toomer. 89.
Giovanni, Nikki. 218.
Go Down, Moses. Folk Songs. 48.
Gonzales, Rodolfo. 234.
Good Times. Lucille Clifton. 193.
"Go through the gates with closed eyes," 122.
"Go 'way from dat window, 'My Honey, My Love!'," 53.
"Grandma sleeps with," 229.
Grandmother. Paula Gunn Allen. 304.
"G'way an' quit dat noise, Miss Lucy—," 79.

Hagedorn, Jessica. 22.
Hahn, Kimiko. 35.
Halfbreed Cry. Wendy Rose. 323.
Harjo, Joy. 339.
Harper, Frances E. W. 63.
Harper, Michael. 205.
Hayden, Robert. 135.
The Heart of a Woman. Georgia Douglas Johnson. 83.
"He awoke this morning uneasily from a dream," 303.
Henderson, David. 207.
He Sees Through Stone. Etheridge Knight. 171.
"He sits at the bar in the Alhambra," 165.
"he was just back," 204.
Homage to the Empress of the Blues. Robert Hayden. 136.
Horne, Frank. 106.
Hospitals Are To Die In. Janice Mirikitani. 42.
Hughes, Langston. 129.
Hunter Mountain. Frank Lima. 245.
"The hunters are back from beating the winter's face," 184.
An Hymn to the Evening. Phillis Wheatley. 62.
"i am here in," 191.
"I am holding this turquoise," 315.
I Am Joaquín, Selections. Rodolfo Gonzales. 234.
"I am rarely vindictive but," 197.
"I am the form that comes to nightwatch," 201.
"I am the smoke king," 65.
"I am tired of work; I am tired of building up somebody," 85.
"I am trying," 106.
"i arrive," 24.
"I climb the black rock mountain," 335.
The Idea of Ancestry. Etheridge Knight. 169.
"I doubt not God is good, well-meaning, kind," 134.
"If I think myself," 174.

"i have all," 223.
"I have known rivers," 130.
"I have learned not to worry about love," 228.
"I have sown beside all waters in my day," 126.
"The imperfection of the world," 177.
Inada, Lawson Fusao. 2.
"In an instant," 241.
In Bondage. Claude McKay. 87.
Indian Song: Survival. Leslie Marmon Silko. 331.
In Medias Res. Frank Lima. 241.
"in my hands, in my eyes, and in myself," 315.
The Insidious Dr. Fu Manchu. Leroi Jones. 174.
In the Barrio. Alurista. 274.
"In the huge, rectangular room, the ceiling," 34.
In the Mourning Time. Robert Hayden. 138.
"In the wintertime," 328.
"In trust you showed me a photograph," 13.
"I reflect on this desperate note," 199.
I Remember. Ricardo Sánchez. 254.
"I see'd her in de Springtime," 59.
I Sit and Sew. Alice Dunbar Nelson. 82.
"is the total black, being spoken," 180.
"I take advantage of inventing women," 244.
"I take my son outside," 316.
"I thought I saw an angel flying low," 127.
"i thought of you," 278.
"It is a new America," 91.
"it is midnight," 190.
I, Too, Sing America. Langston Hughes. 131.
It Was a Funky Deal. Etheridge Knight. 173.
"it was a long," 202.
"it was very pleasant," 218.
"it was wild," 212.
"It will rain forever here," 242.

"i used to dream militant," 222.
"I've come this far to freedom and I won't turn back," 164.
I Want To Die while You Love Me. Georgia Douglas Johnson. 84.
I Was Always Fascinated. Alma Villanueva. 266.
"I would be wandering in distant fields," 87.
Jazzonia. Langston Hughes. 129.
Jitterbugs. Leroi Jones. 177.
John Henry. Folk Songs. 54.
Johnson, Fenton. 85.
Johnson, Georgia Douglas. 83.
Johnson, James Weldon. 67.
Jones, Leroi. 174.
Jordan, June. 194.
Kaufman, Bob. 185.
Kicking Lego Blocks, Selections. Shawn Wong. 14.
"A knife blade of cold air keeps prying," 167.
Knight, Etheridge. 169.
Kopis'taya (a Gathering of Spirits). Paula Gunn Allen. 305.
Kuo, Alex. 6.
"Language is movement," 339.
Last Look at La Plata, Missouri. Jim Barnes. 298.
Last Poem I'm Gonna Write about Us. Sonia Sanchez. 189.
Lee, Don L. 210.
Legacy: My South. Dudley Randall. 154.
The Legendary Storm. Lawson Fusao Inada. 3.
Let My People Go. James Weldon Johnson. 68.
The Liar. Leroi Jones. 175.
Life for My Child Is Simple and Is Good. Gwendolyn Brooks. 162.
Lima, Frank. 241.
"Limping to this spreading portrait," 7.
Little Brown Baby. Paul Laurence Dunbar. 77.
Long Person. Gladys Cardiff. 319.
Lorde, Audre. 180.

Lost in Sulphur Canyons. Jim Barnes. 299.
Love among Friends. Shawn Wong. 13.
Love Poem. Leslie Marmon Silko. 336.
Madgett, Naomi Long. 163.
Major, Clarence. 199.
Many a Thousand Die. Folk Songs. 52.
Mar, Laureen. 32.
McKay, Claude. 86.
Medicine. Alice Walker. 229.
Middle Passage. Robert Hayden. 142.
Midway. Naomi Long Madgett. 164.
Mirikitani, Janice. 39.
Mixed Sketches. Don L. Lee. 210.
Momaday, N. Scott. 301.
Mortality. Naomi Long Madgett. 163.
Mother's Habits. Nikki Giovanni. 223.
"My Daddy has paid the rent," 193.
"my first vivid memory of you," 259.
"My little stone," 108.
My Mother Pieced Quilts. Teresa Palomo Acosta. 285.
My Mother, Who Came from China, Where She Never Saw Snow. Laureen Mar. 34.
"My hair is springy like the forest grasses," 166.
"My people cry ashes," 323.
The Negro Speaks of Rivers. Langston Hughes. 130.
Nelson, Alice Dunbar. 82.
New Face. Alice Walker. 228.
Niatum, Duane. 303.
The Night-Blooming Cereus. Robert Hayden. 139.
"No hay nada nuevo en nueva york," 268.
"No more driver call for me," 52.
Nocturne at Bethesda. Arna Bontemps. 127.
None of It Was. Clarence Major. 202.
Notes Found Near a Suicide. Frank Horne. 108.
O Black and Unknown Bards. James Weldon Johnson. 67.
O Daedalus, Fly Away Home. Robert Hayden. 135.

"Oh, silver tree!," 129.
On Being Brought from Africa to America. Phillis Wheatley. 61.
"Once more, listening to the wind and rain," 124.
159 John Street. Frank Lima. 242.
"One thing I don't need," 230.
"One thing you left with us, Jack Johnson," 117.
"Only our hearts will argue hard," 196.
"On ochre walls in ice-formed caves shaggy Neanderthals," 185.
"or: he even stopped for green lights," 216.
Ortiz, Simon. 314.
"Out of her own body she pushed," 304.
"The park, the heart, you see at town's center is soft," 298.
Pennsylvania Dutch Country. Sonia Sanchez. 192.
Pietri, Pedro. 256.
Piñero, Miguel. 268.
Plena. Frank Lima. 248.
Plucking Out a Rhythm. Lawson Fusao Inada. 4.
Poem at Thirty. Sonia Sanchez. 190.
Poem No. 4. Sonia Sanchez. 191.
A Poem Some People Will Have To Understand. Leroi Jones. 178.
Poor Mouse. Mei-mei Berssenbrugge. 10.
"Poplars are standing there still as death," 123.
Portrait of a Negative. Alex Kuo. 7.
"Pour, O pour that parting soul in song," 90.
"the prairie tries to eat the forest," 297.
The Prisoners. Robert Hayden. 153.
"Rain smell comes with the wind," 336.
Randall, Dudley. 154.
The Rattlesnake Band. Robert J. Conley. 307.
Reapers. Jean Toomer. 88.

The Return. Arna Bontemps. 124.
Revolutionary Dreams. Nikki Giovanni. 222.
Right On: Wite America. Sonia Sanchez. 187.
Rodríguez, Aleida. 279.
Roman Poem Number Thirteen. June Jordan. 196.
Rose, Wendy. 323.
Runagate Runagate. Robert Hayden. 150.
"Runs falls rises stumbles on from darkness into darkness," 150.
Russell, Norman. 296.
"Sails flashing to the wind like weapons," 142.
"The sale began—young girls were there," 63.
Sánchez, Ricardo. 249.
Sanchez, Sonia. 187.
The Second Sermon on the Warpland. Gwendolyn Brooks. 160.
"seeing good places," 334.
The Serenity in Stones. Simon Ortiz. 315.
The Sermon on the Warpland. Gwendolyn Brooks. 159.
Shange, Ntozake. 230.
She Hugged Me and Kissed Me. Folk Songs. 59.
Silko, Leslie Marmon. 328.
Simple. Naomi Long Madgett. 165.
"The sky has the luxury of going anywhere," 245.
"The sky, lazily disdaining to pursue," 89.
The Slave Auction. Frances E. W. Harper. 63.
Snag. Victor Hernandez Cruz. 278.
"some," 189.
"Some nights the moon is the curve of a comb," 32.
Someone Talking. Joy Harjo. 339.
Song. Folk Songs. 52.
Song for My Father. Jessica Hagedorn. 24.
The Song of Bullets. Jessica Hagedorn. 29.

The Song of the Smoke. W.E.B. Du Bois. 65.
Song of the Son. Jean Toomer. 90.
Song to the Runaway Slave. Folk Songs. 53.
Song Without Words. Pedro Pietri. 256.
"Soon as the sun forsook the eastern main," 62.
Sorcery. Jessica Hagedorn. 22.
The Source. Lawson Fusao Inada. 2.
Southern Mansion. Arna Bontemps. 123.
The Southern Road. Dudley Randall. 155.
Spring Street Bar. Mei-mei Berssenbrugge. 12.
"Start with a simple room—," 4.
Steal Away. Folk Songs. 51.
"Steel doors—guillotine gates—," 153.
"The stories," 325.
Story Keeper. Wendy Rose. 325.
Strange Legacies. Sterling Brown. 117.
Strong Men. Sterling Brown. 119.
Summer Oracle. Audre Lorde. 182.
Summer Wish. Frank Lima. 244.
Sunday, August 11, 1974. Miguel Algarín. 283.
"Sundays too my father got up early," 149.
Survival This Way. Simon Ortiz. 314.
Swing Low, Sweet Chariot. Folk Songs. 50.
"Taped to the wall of my cell are 47 pictures: 47 black," 169.
That's How I Was. Carlos Conde. 291.
"there are some people i know," 22.
There Is a Hungry Watching. Norman Russell. 297.
There Is Nothing New in New York. Miguel Piñero. 268.
"There the black river, boundary to hell," 155.
"They dragged you from the homeland," 119.
"They eat beans mostly, this old yellow pair," 158.

"They finally," 42.
"They have fenced in the dirt road," 225.
"they were just meant as covers," 285.
"this country might have," 187.
"this is has to be here," 203.
"this is power," 192.
"This is the debt I pay," 76.
"This is the surest death," 163.
"This is the urgency: Live!" 160.
"This is the Wheel of Dreams," 301.
Those Winter Sundays. Robert Hayden. 149.
3 AM. Joy Harjo. 342.
The Time We Climbed Snake Mountain. Leslie Marmon Silko. 334.
Tired. Fenton Johnson. 85.
"Today I love you so much I mistrust you -," 11.
Today Is a Day of Great Joy. Victor Hernandez Cruz. 276.
Toe'osh: A Laguna Coyote Story. Leslie Marmon Silko. 328.
To Insure Survival. Simon Ortiz. 317.
To Jesus Villanueva, with Love. Alma Villanueva. 259.
Tolson, Melvin B. 96.
To My Son Parker, Asleep in the Next Room. Bob Kaufman. 185.
"Tonight," 195.
Toomer, Jean. 88.
Toward. Ricardo Sánchez. 249.
The Tree Sleeps in the Winter. Norman Russell. 296.
The Tropics in New York. Claude McKay. 86.
"'Twas mercy brought me from my *Pagan* land," 61.
"Two hours after I saw her," 14.
"u feel that way sometimes," 210.
Untitled. Alma Villaneuva. 263.
Upstate. Derek Walcott. 167.
Vacations. Frank Lima. 243.
Vietnam. Clarence Major. 204.
Villanueva, Alma. 259.
Waiting in the Children's Hospital. Clarence Major. 199.
Walcott, Derek. 167.

Walker, Alice. 224.
Walk. Frank Horne. 106.
Walk with De Mayor of Harlem. David Henderson. 207.
The Way the Bird Sat. Ray Young Bear. 337.
We Assume: On the Death of Our Son, Reuben Masai Harper. Michael Harper. 205.
"weaver," 292.
"We have lost the planet to the block party," 243.
Welch, James. 312.
"We raise de wheat," 52.
Were You There When They Crucified My Lord?. Folk Songs. 60.
"we run the dangercourse," 213.
"We took the mouse alive," 10.
We Wait. Robert J. Conley. 309.
We Walk the Way of the New World. Don L. Lee. 213.
We Wear the Mask. Paul Laurence Dunbar. 75.
"We went north," 331.
"What desperate nightmare rapts me to this land," 154.
What for?/Pa'Victor Hara. Alurista. 270.
"what for the rush," 270.
"What happens to a dream deferred?," 132.
What I Tell Him. Simon Ortiz. 316.
"What I thought was love," 175.
Wheatley, Phillis. 61.
When I Nap. Nikki Giovanni. 219.
"When it is finally ours, this freedom, this liberty, this beautiful," 137.
"When John Henry was a little fellow," 54.
When Malindy Sings. Paul Laurence Dunbar. 79.
When Raza?. Alurista. 275.
"when they stop poems," 276.
"When they woke me," 318.
When Was the Last Time You Saw Mami Smile?. Americo Casiano. 288.

When You Have Forgotten Sunday: The Love Story. Gwendolyn Brooks. 156.
Where Mountain Lion Lay Down with Deer. Leslie Marmon Silko. 335.
The Window Frames the Moon. Laureen Mar. 32.
"the windows of these thoughts," 256.
"Without expectation," 182.
The Woman Thing. Audre Lorde. 184.
The Women Gather. Nikki Giovanni. 220.

Wong, Shawn. 13.
Yellowstone. Frank Lima. 247.
"Yesterday," 39.
Yet Do I Marvel. Countee Cullen. 134.
"you cannot leave," 263.
"You come forth," 317.
Young Soul. Leroi Jones. 179.
"You sang round-dance songs," 322.
"You see, the problem is," 312.
"Your mother poses on black rocks," 33.

ACKNOWLEDGEMENTS

Permission to reprint copyrighted poems is gratefully acknowledged to the following:

PAULA GUNN ALLEN, for "Kopis'taya" from *Songs from This Earth on Turtle's Back*, Joseph Bruchac, ed. "Grandmother" from *Coyote's Daylight Trip* by Paula Gunn Allen. Copyright © by Paula Gunn Allen.

ALURISTA, for "In the Barrio"; "What For?/pa'victor hara" and "When raza?" Copyright © by Alurista.

BEACON PRESS, for "For Christopher"; "All the World Moved"; "Roman Poem Number Thirteen" and "About the Reunion" from *Things That I Do in the Dark: Selected Poems* by June Jordan. Copyright © 1977 by June Jordan.

MEI-MEI BERSSENBRUGGE, for "Poor Mouse" and "Fish and Swimmers" from *Summits Move with the Tide* by Mei-mei Berssenbrugge. "Spring Street Bar" from *Random Possession* by Mei-mei Berssenbrugge. Copyright © by Mei-mei Berssenbrugge.

BROADSIDE PRESS, for "The Idea of Ancestry"; "He Sees Through Stone" and "It Was a Funky Deal" from *Poems from Prison* by Etheridge Knight. Copyright © 1968 by Etheridge Knight. "Last Song I'm Gonna Write About Us" from *We a Bad People* by Sonia Sanchez. Copyright © 1970 by Sonia Sanchez. "But He Was Cool" and "Assassination" from *Don't Cry, Scream* by Don L. Lee. Copyright © 1969 by Don L. Lee. "Mixed Sketches" and "We Walk the Way of the New World" from *We Walk the Way of the New World* by Don L. Lee. Copyright © 1970 by Don L. Lee. "Legacy: My South" and "The Southern Road" by Dudley Randall. Copyright © by Dudley Randall.

GWENDOLYN BROOKS, for "The Bean Eaters"; "Life for My Child Is Simple and Good"; "When You have Forgotten Sunday: The Love Story"; "The Sermon on the Warpland" and "The

Second Sermon on the Warpland". Copyright © by Gwendolyn Brooks.

JOSEPH BRUCHAC, for "Coming Back." Copyright © by Joseph Bruchac.

ROBERT CONLEY, for "The Rattlesnake Band" and "We Wait." Copyright © by Robert Conley.

DODD, MEAD & COMPANY, INC., for "Dark Symphony" from *Rendezvous with America* by Melvin B. Tolson. Copyright 1944 by Dodd, Mead & Company, Inc. Copyright renewed 1972 by Ruth S. Tolson.

E.P. DUTTON, a division of NEW AMERICAN LIBRARY, for "Walk with De Mayor of Harlem" from *De Mayor of Harlem* by David Henderson. Copyright © 1965, 1967, 1969, 1970 by David Henderson.

FARRAR, STRAUS AND GIROUX, INC., for "Upstate" from *The Fortunate Traveller* by Derek Walcott. Copyright © 1980, 1981 by Derek Walcott. "Upstate" originally appeared in *The New Yorker*.

RODOLFO GONZALES, for selections from "I Am Joaquin." Copyright © 1967 by Rodolfo Gonzales.

JESSICA HAGEDORN, for "The Song of Bullets". The poem has appeared in *Art Against Apartheid* and *Open Places*. Copyright © by Jessica Hagedorn.

KIMIKO HAHN, for "The Bath, August 6, 1945" and "Daughter". Copyright © by Kimiko Hahn.

HARCOURT BRACE JOVANOVICH, INC., for "Expect Nothing," copyright © 1972 by Alice Walker. "Burial," copyright © 1970 by Alice Walker. "New Face," copyright © 1973 by Alice Walker. Poems from REVOLUTIONARY PETUNIAS AND OTHER POEMS. "Medicine" from ONCE. Copyright © 1968 by Alice Walker.

JOY HARJO, for "3 A.M." from *What Moon Drove Me to This?* by Joy Harjo and "Someone Talking." Copyright © by Joy Harjo.

HAROLD OBER ASSOCIATES, INC., for "The Return"; "A Black Man Talks of Reaping"; "Southern Mansion"; "Close Your Eyes" and "Nocturne at Bethesda" by Arna Bontemps. Copyright © 1963 by Arna Bontemps.

HARPER & ROW, PUBLISHERS, INC., for "Yet Do I Marvel" from *On These I Stand* by Countee Cullen. Copyright 1925 by Harper & Row, Publishers, Inc. Renewed 1953 by Ida M. Cullen. "Blue Like Death" from *Riding the Earthboy 40* revised edition by James Welch. Copyright © 1971, 1976 by James Welch. "Strange Legacies" and "Strong Men" from *The Collected Poems of Sterling A. Brown* selected by Michael S. Harper. Copyright © 1980 by Sterling A. Brown. "Carriers of the Dream Wheel" and "Earth and I Gave You Turquoise" from *The Gourd Dancer* by N. Scott Momaday. Copyright © 1975 by N. Scott Momaday.

INDIANA UNIVERSITY PRESS, for "I Want to Die While You Love Me" and "The Heart of Woman" by Georgia Douglas Johnson. "I Sit and Sew" by Alice Dunbar Nelson. Poems from *Black Sister*, edited by Erlene Stetson. Copyright © 1981 by Erlene Stetson.

THE JUNIOR LEAGUE OF SEATTLE, for "Combing" by Gladys Cardiff from *Puget Soundings*, 1971. Copyright © by Gladys Cardiff.

ALFRED A. KNOPF, INC., for "Jazzonia" from *The Weary Blues* by Langston Hughes. Copyright 1926 by Alfred A. Knopf, Inc. and renewed 1954 by Langston Hughes. "The Negro Speaks of Rivers" and "I, Too" from *Selected Poems of Langston Hughes*. Copyright 1926 by Alfred A. Knopf, Inc., and renewed 1954 by Langston Hughes. "Dreams Deferred" and "Freedom" from *The Panther and the Lash: Poems of Our Times* by Langston Hughes. Copyright © 1967 by Arna Bontemps and George Houston Bass.

ALEX KUO, for "Portrait of a Negative" from *New Letters from Hiroshima and Other Poems* by Alex Kuo. "Did You Not See" from *Changing the River* by Alex Kuo. Copyright © by Alex Kuo.

LIVERIGHT PUBLISHING CORPORATION, for "Reapers," "Georgia Dusk," "Brown River Smile" and "Song of the Son" from *Cane* by Jean Toomer. Copyright 1923 by Boni & Liveright. Copyright renewed 1951 by Jean Toomer. "In Medias Res"; "159 John Street"; "Vacations"; "Summer Wish"; "Hunter Mountain"; "Yellowstone" and "Plena" from *Angel* by Frank Lima. Copyright

© 1975, 1976 by the Liveright Publishing Corporation. "Middle Passage"; "Those Winter Sundays"; "Nightblooming Cereus"; "Runagate Runagate"; "Prisoners"; "O Daedalus, Fly Away Home"; "Homage to the Empress of the Blues" and "Frederick Douglas" from *Angle of Ascent: New and Selected Poems* by Robert Hayden. Copyright © 1975, 1972, 1970, 1966 by Robert Hayden. "In the Mourning Time" from *Words in the Mourning Time* by Robert Hayden. Copyright © 1970 by Robert Hayden.

MACMILLAN PUBLISHING COMPANY, for two excerpts from *For Colored Girls Who Have Considered Suicide/When the Rainbow is Enuf* by Ntozake Shange. Copyright © 1975, 1976, 1977 by Ntozake Shange.

NAOMI LONG MADGETT, for "Midway" and "Mortality" from *Star By Star* by Naomi Long Madgett. "Simple" and "Black Woman" from *Pink Ladies in the Afternoon* by Naomi Long Madgett. Copyright © by Naomi Long Madgett.

CLARENCE MAJOR, for "Dismal Moment, Passing" and "Form." Copyright © by Clarence Major.

LAUREEN MAR, for "My Mother, Who Came from China, Where She Never Saw Snow," "Black Rocks," and "The Window Frames the Moon." Copyright © by Laureen Mar.

JANICE MIRIKITANI, for "August 6"; "Desert Flowers"; and "Hospitals Are To Die In" from *Awake in the River* by Janice Mirikitani. Copyright © 1978 by Janice Mirikitani.

MOMO'S PRESS, for "Song For My Father" and "Sorcery" from *Dangerous Music* by Jessica Hagedorn. Copyright © by Jessica Hagedorn.

NEW DIRECTIONS PUBLISHING CORPORATION, for "To My Son Parker Asleep in the Next Room," from *Solitudes Crowded With Loneliness* by Bob Kaufman. Copyright © by Bob Kaufman.

THE NEW YORK QUARTERLY, for "Farewell" by Liz Sohappy Bahe.

DUANE NIATUM, for "Chief Leschi of the Nisqually." Copyright © by Duane Niatum.

NORTHWEST REVIEW, for "Long Person" by Gladys Cardiff.

Copyright © by Gladys Cardiff. "The Way the Bird Sat" by Ray A. Young Bear. Copyright © by Ray A. Young Bear. Poems appeared in Vol. 13, no. 2.

W.W. NORTON AND COMPANY, for "Coal" and "The Womanthing" from *Coal* by Audre Lorde. Copyright © 1968, 1970, 1976 by Audre Lorde. "Summer Oracle" from *The Black Unicorn* by Audre Lorde. Copyright © by Audre Lorde

SIMON ORTIZ, for "What I Tell Him"; "To Insure Survival"; "The Serenity in Stones" and "Survival This Way." Copyright © by Simon Ortiz.

RANDOM HOUSE, INC., for "today is a day of great joy" and "snag" from *Snaps* by Victor Hernandez Cruz. Copyright © 1968, 1969 by Victor Hernandez Cruz. "Good Times" from *Good Times* by Lucille Clifton. Copyright © 1969 by Lucille Clifton.

ALEIDA RODRIGUEZ, for "Exploraciones/Bronchitis: The Rosario Beach House." Copyright © by Aleida Rodriguez.

NORMAN H. RUSSELL, for "The Tree Sleeps in Winter" and "There Is a Hungry Watch". Copyright © by Norman H. Russell.

RICARDO SÁNCHEZ, for "Toward" and "I Remember." Copyright © by Ricardo Sánchez.

SONIA SANCHEZ, for "Poem at Thirty," "Poem No. 4," "Pennsylvania Dutch Country," and "Right On: White America." Copyright © by Sonia Sanchez.

MELVIN B. TOLSON, JR., for "African China" by Melvin B. Tolson. Copyright © by Melvin B. Tolson.

TWAYNE PUBLISHERS, a division of G.K. HALL & CO., for "Tropics in New York" and "In Bondage" from *Selected Poems of Claude McKay* by Claude McKay. Copyright 1981 by Twayne Publishers, a division of G.K. Hall & Co., Boston.

UNIVERSITY OF ILLINOIS PRESS, for "We Assume: On the Death of Our Son, Reuben Masai Harper" from *Images of Kin: New and Selected Poems* by Michael S. Harper. Copyright © 1970, 1971, 1972, 1973, 1974, 1975, 1976, 1977 by Michael S. Harper. "Lost in Sulphur Canyons" and "Last Look at La Plata, Missouri" from *The American Book of the Dead* by Jim Barnes. Copyright © 1982 by Jim Barnes.

UNIVERSITY OF SOUTHERN CALIFORNIA PRESS, for "My Mother Pieced Quilts" by Teresa Acosta Paloma, from *Festival de Flor y Canto: An Anthology of Chicano Literature*, edited by Alurista, *et al*. Copyright 1976 by El Centro Chicano, University of Southern California.

VIKING PENGUIN, INC., for "Let My People Go" from *God's Trombones* by James Weldon Johnson. Copyright 1927 by The Viking Press, Inc. Copyright renewed © 1955 by Grace Nail Johnson. "O Black and Unknown Bards" from *St. Peter Relates an Accident* by James Weldon Johnson. Copyright 1935 by James Weldon Johnson. Copyright renewed © 1963 by Grace Nail Johnson.

ALMA VILLNUEVA, for "I Was Always Fascinated," "To Jesus Villanueva, with Love" and "Untitled". Copyright © by Alma Villanueva.

WESLEYAN UNIVERSITY PRESS, for "Vietnam"; "Waiting in the Children's Hospital" and "None of It Was" from *Swallow the Lake* by Clarence Major. Copyright © 1970 by Clarence Major.

WEST END PRESS, for "Story Keeper" and "Halfbreed Cry" from *The Halfbreed Chronicles and Other Poems* by Wendy Rose. Copyright © 1985 by Wendy Rose.

WILLIAM MORROW & COMPANY, for "The Insidious Dr. Fu Manchu"; "The Liar"; "Cold Term II"; "Jitterbugs"; "A Poem Some People Will Have to Understand" and "Young Soul" from *Selected Poetry of Amiri Baraka/Leroi Jones*. Copyright © 1961, 1969, 1979 by Amiri Baraka. "The Women Gather"; "Revolutionary Dreams" and "Mother's Habits" from *The Women and the Men* by Nikki Giovanni. Copyright © 1970, 1974, 1975 by Nikki Giovanni. "A Certain Peace [9 jan. 72]" and "When I Nap" from *My House* by Nikki Giovanni. Copyright © 1972 by Nikki Giovanni. "Plucking Out a Rhythm"; "The Source" and "The Legendary Storm" from *Before the War* by Lawson Fusao Inada. Copyright © 1971 by Lawson Fusao Inada. "Blanket Weaver" by Sandra Maria Esteves. Copyright © 1975 by Sandra Maria Esteves. "There Is Nothing New in New York" by Miguel Pinero. Copyright © 1975 by Miguel Pinero. "Songs Without Words" and "Do Not Let" by

Pedro Pietri. Copyright © 1975 by Pedro Pietri. "That's How I was" by Carlos Conde. Copyright © 1975 by Carlos Conde. "When Was the Last Time You Saw Mami Smile" by Americo Casiano. Copyright © 1975 by Americo Casiano. "Sunday, August 11, 1974" by Miguel Algarin. Copyright © 1975 by Miguel Algarin. From *Nuyorican Poetry*, edited by Miguel Algarin and Miguel Pinero. Copyright © 1975 by Miguel Algarin and Miguel Pinero.

SHAWN WONG, for "Love Among Friends" and excerpt from "Kicking Lego Blocks". Copyright © by Shawn Wong.